Growing Together

**Six
Intergenerational
Celebrations**

Volume I
Fall & Winter

**with contributions by
Kathy Finley
Sylvia DeVillers
Rita Mailander
Kathy Coffey**

 Living the Good News
a division of The Morehouse Group

An Acknowledgment

Growing Together incorporates the work of many unnamed contributors, as well as those listed here. We wish to acknowledge the many editors, writers, staff members and others whose vision, ideas and words enrich this resource for parish families.

© 1999 Living the Good News, Inc.

Cover illustration: Teresa Flavin
Cover design: Jim Lemons
Illustrations: Sally Brewer Lawrence, Anne Kosel, Victoria Bergesen
Editor: Dina Strong Gluckstern

Scripture texts referred to in this work are taken from the New Revised Standard Version Bible, copyright © 1989 by the Division of Christian Education of the National Council of Churches of Christ in the USA, and are used by permission.

ISBN: 1-889108-45-6

Table of Contents

Introduction

Since our earliest days, Living the Good News has encouraged parishes to bring all ages together to worship, celebrate and learn. Through such occasions we can become better acquainted with our parish family, young and old together. We can take steps toward making our parish the warm, nurturing community we long for in our fragmented world. Older adults who grew up in the pre-Vatican II Church sometimes feel a sense of displacement in parish life today. Celebrations and rituals help members of every generation find individual meaning in a common ground of experience.

Through celebrations, we can experience scripture and traditions in a fresh way that can give beauty and meaning to our daily lives. In this volume of *Growing Together* we offer suggestions for organizing six sessions focusing on:
- Building a Parish Family
- All Saints
- Thanksgiving
- Advent
- Christmas
- Epiphany

In each chapter you will find *far more than enough activities for a one-hour session.* This abundance allows you to choose only those activities that meet your parish's particular needs and fit its schedule.

Our hope is that, in a small way, this book will help the Body of Christ grow in understanding and "build itself up through love" (Ephesians 4:16).

Why Gather All Ages Together?

Many of our experiences in life happen when several generations are together. Vacations, trips, holidays and family events are shared by old and young alike. We tend to separate people by ages mainly for education and employment.

Many parish programs make this same separation of generations, but more and more catechists and religious educators are recommending programs in which adults and children learn together.

Growing Together is designed to meet the need for generations to learn together. This approach requires that we venture beyond traditional learning methods into the world of experiential learning.

What Is Experiential Learning?

In *Growing Together* you will find ideas for experiences that involve the whole person rather than the intellect alone. These experiences include, but are by no means limited to, art, movement activities, writing simple poems, making quick paper banners and various outreach projects.

Growing Together

Experiential learning is the way we learn in real life. It is the way that young children acquire an amazing "data base" of skills and information in the first few years of life. (From ages 2 to 4, our vocabularies alone grow from about 50 words to 10,000 or more.) Experiential learning is how we learned to speak and how any of us have learned most of what we know.

Experiential learning takes us beyond a nodding acquaintance with new ideas and allows us to make them our own. Though it does not rely heavily on such methods as reciting, taking notes on a lecture or writing objective answers in blanks, neither is it incapable of communicating objective, factual information. The activities in *Growing Together* are balanced to teach specific content *and* evoke intuitive, feeling responses.

You have probably heard the maxim: I hear and I forget; I see and I remember; I do and I understand. The more of ourselves (body, mind and spirit) we can use to explore an idea, the more the idea becomes our own.

Similarly, Jesus understood that the more of ourselves we bring into relationship with God, the more intimate and enduring this relationship becomes. He taught that we are not far from the kingdom of heaven if we love God with all our hearts, all our souls, all our minds and all our strength.

Thus, experiential learning in a Christian setting beckons us to sing, dance and clap. It beckons us to construct a scale model or act out a skit. It beckons us to play. We use experiential methods because they:

- rely on other modalities of learning rather than the intellect alone.
- involve the whole person: senses, emotions, mind and spirit.
- make learning a thing to enjoy and internalize.
- provide opportunities for students to discover and use their talents, to learn to work together harmoniously and to develop skills of leadership and creativity.
- welcome the Holy Spirit to lead us to unexpected insights.

Experiential methods require careful planning and sometimes more effort than preparing a lecture. But inviting parish members to participate fully in their own education can produce a rich harvest of responsible attitudes, sound conceptual learning and joy for both catechists and students.

When Can You Use These Sessions?

In a typical parish, consider using these sessions as:

- parish intergenerational programs.
- seasonal parish family gatherings.
- primary religious education material for a small parish.
- supplementary material for large parish religious education programs.
- supplementary material for religion classes in Catholic schools.
- home-study religious education programs.

- RCIA gatherings for adults and children.
- catechetical sessions for children preparing for Christian Initiation.
- small Christian communities or base communities.
- incorporation into family sacramental programs.

Finding time and resources to add another component to already full schedules, both in families and in parish organizations, can be a challenge. Family-centered gatherings and Christian Initiation groups of all kinds have fewer constraints in following tightly scheduled curriculums.

Look to different groups in the parish who could successfully host an intergenerational gathering. One promising lead would be to invite parish youth organizations to be in charge of leading one or more sessions. Consider also the possibility of asking a different parish organization to host a session. Use our session planning pages as an organizing tool for host teams.

How Do You Plan a Session?

In each chapter of *Growing Together* you will find several **Key Ideas** and a cluster of activities that teach each **Key Idea**. When planning a one-hour session, *you will need to choose only a few of these activities*. Ask yourself:

- Which key ideas in this chapter are most important for our parish to explore?
- Which of the suggested activities will best help us to explore these key ideas?
- Which activities best fit our schedule?
- Which activities best fit the diverse ages and learning styles of our congregation?

What Materials Will You Need?

We know that not every parish can allocate generous funds for Christian education. We welcome the educational potential of such equipment as video cameras and tape recorders, but we do not assume all parishes can afford them. The materials called for in this book are simple and inexpensive.

Each activity includes a list of materials needed. Materials common to many *Growing Together* sessions include:

> Bibles
> chalkboard and chalk or newsprint
>   and marker
> felt pens
> crayons, regular and oversized
>   for young children
> drawing paper
> glue
> scissors

How Can Prayer Play a Lively Part?

Most of us have had rich experiences with corporate prayer in the context of our parish worship. Many of us also have private prayer lives that nourish us, deepening our relationship to God and to our innermost selves.

For some of us this private prayer time is structured and consistent in time and place. For others it may be spontaneous and less formal. Fewer of us have prayed together comfortably and spontaneously with other members of our parish in an informal setting. A true blessing of parish gatherings with all ages together is the growing ability to pray together, rejoicing in the presence of God and God's people gathered.

You can begin your parish family sessions with prayer and close with prayer. As a sense of community begins to develop through working together, certain moments will call forth the desire to pray together right then with no worry as to having just the proper words.

Here are various suggestions for closing prayers; you will find more at the end of each chapter.

- Plan your session with time for unhurried prayer. Do not worry if the younger children prefer to wander around at this time. They will still hear and be part of the prayer.
- Pass out songbooks and sing together as a closing prayer.
- Supply small pieces of paper, pencils and a basket. As people arrive, invite them to write prayer requests on the slips of paper and place them in the basket. At the end of the session the leader includes the prayer requests in the closing prayer.
- Bring into the center of your prayer circle the fruits of your session: the art work created, props used in a skit, etc. Ask the group to quietly reflect on insights they have gained from the session. As leader, offer your own thanksgivings and allow time for others to do likewise.

- Once you sense that people want to offer their thoughts aloud, here is a simple, safe way to invite extemporaneous prayers. Form a circle with everyone holding hands. Explain that you are going to offer a brief prayer and that when you are finished, you will squeeze the hand of the person to your right. That person either offers a prayer aloud or chooses to remain silent, then squeezes the hand of the next person as a signal for the next person to continue.
- Invite a small group of volunteers to spend a few minutes with you preparing the closing prayer. This prayer can take the form of music, dance, art or even mime. Or one of the activities a small group completed during your session could be presented to your whole parish family as a prayer.

How Can You Group the Participants?

One satisfying way to group participants in parish family sessions is by offering a choice of activities, each in its own room or corner. Prepare half-a-dozen activities for your session, and briefly present the choices to the participants. Ask participants to choose more than one activity, so that you can rotate the groups during the hour.

One parish using this method allowed participants to choose freely between several activities: watching a film made by intermediate participants, decorating a processional cross, discussing the day's liturgical rites, conducting a movement session (especially appropriate for the youngest children) and learning a hymn appropriate for the day.

Another method is to break into temporary and arbitrary groups as needed for particular activities. This can be done by counting off, by color of name tags, month of birthday or in some other way.

Some parishes have felt more secure with long-term groups. Some make pairs of an adult and a child and then form groups by combining pairs. Other parishes have established "families" or "tribes" of mixed ages who work together on group assignments.

How Can You Integrate Children Into Parish Family Sessions?

Successful parish family programs help children to be participants, not onlookers. Planning must therefore take into account children's learning needs, their limited reading skills, spoken vocabularies, dexterity and attention spans. The activities and methods of presentation should be chosen with these things in mind.

Since you want the children to be integrated into the group, you will *not* want to provide child-size tables and chairs. You *will* want to encourage everyone to help the children see, hear and take part.

For example, if each person is to write something on a 3" x 5" card, some adult should write what a youngster wants to say. If you plan to make drawings, it helps to provide crayons of both regular and kindergarten size.

When an activity calls for oral answers or group discussion, the leader will want to be careful to protect the children's right to participate. The leader should caution adults not to put words in the children's mouths, answer for them or ignore them.

If your session includes preschoolers, you may want to set up a corner with paper and crayons, play dough and blocks. Then as the session unfolds, the children can choose whether to work in their own corner or to participate with the larger group. You will most likely find that the adults enjoy and learn much from the fresh outlook and abounding faith of the children.

What Activities Work Best for All Ages Together?

Brainstorming

Often an activity will say "Brainstorm a list of ways to…" or "Brainstorm the kinds of feelings you have when…"

Brainstorming means having everyone throw out ideas in rapid succession. Be sure everyone knows that the rules of the game are:
- Do not judge or evaluate ideas.
- Do not wait to be called on; just speak up.
- Add on to what others say.

The leader or someone else should list all ideas on chalkboard or newsprint. The values of brainstorming are:
- It gets everyone to offer ideas.

Growing Together

- Some "way-out" ideas often can lead to a fresh way to look at something.
- It is a good way to get people to open up and start talking.
- If you are looking for a way to do something, you may find it by combining several ideas from the list.

If you need to teach a group how to brainstorm, you might explain the process and then let members try it on a topic such as "How many ways can we use a newspaper?"

Drama, Dance, Movement

Creative movement, dance, drama, mime and story telling are excellent ways to present scripture in parish family sessions. Another approach is "readers' theater," the dramatic reading of a story from scripture by a narrator and others who read the parts of the various characters. (You might want to give the audience a part as well, maybe sound effects or cheering for the hero!)

Some of the activities in *Growing Together* suggest dramatizations of incidents from scripture, with the players making up their own dialogue. These informal skits provide an enjoyable way for participants to see the details, as well as the emotional content, of an incident. At other times, groups are asked to plan and present a brief skit on some real life situation related to a key idea.

In a parish family session, drama in all its forms should be done in a spontaneous fashion—no memorizing of lines or elaborate props and costumes. Encourage participants to project themselves into the scene and to use their own words to express feelings and ideas. If a group chooses to put a biblical event in a modern setting, welcome current idioms of speech and humor.

Enjoying a learning experience makes it a memorable encounter. Humor is one key; sometimes laughing at human folly produces that "Ah-ha!" experience, when suddenly we come to a new realization about ourselves.

Dramatized stories, concepts taught through movement, parables enacted in modern settings—all communicate the word in lively, engaging fashion. Incorporating the dramatic arts in Christian education helps us discover that we are indeed co-creators with God.

These methods allow all ages to work, talk, play and create together. They provide an arena in which individuals may express who they really are. Such a shared experience engages us directly with scripture, evoking insights that can inspire significant change and growth.

Music

"Make a joyful noise to the Lord, all the lands! Serve the Lord with gladness! Come into his presence with singing!" (Psalm 100:1)

Quiet, peaceful music draws us into a prayerful attitude, while bright, rousing music stirs us to express joy and praise. Music belongs to all phases of Christian celebration, but especially in parish family sessions. It is a medium that appeals to old and young alike. It can set the mood for a session, or change the mood to prepare for a change of activity.

Sometimes you may want to invite youngsters to teach a song they have learned in their class. You can invite music ministers to teach a song or to lead a hymn-sing. You can ask volunteers to prepare a mime, a movement activity or a liturgical dance to accompany a song sung by the whole parish family.

To encourage singing, use songs familiar to the participants. If children are participating, you can coordinate the music with that used in their parish religious education classes.

Art

Art is an important channel through which all ages may express their understandings, beliefs and feelings. In fact, through participation in art, a person's understandings may deepen and come into focus. Many people can express ideas more readily in a visual way than by verbal means. Not least of all, art in individual or cooperative form can be satisfying and fun.

The attitudes with which art activities are handled will in great measure affect the participants' responses. Acceptance of everyone's art, based on respect for individual and developmental differences, is essential.

Encourage creativity. (Coloring within the lines is not important!) Take care not to impose your own way of seeing the world on others, avoiding competition and comparison. Ask everyone to try the art activities, explaining that in this setting, producing a great work of art is not important.

Creating something of meaning to one's self is the object. (A work of art that opens a new door to its maker may also speak to others in your parish family.) Creating art may also be an act of worship.

Parish family members will be more likely to experiment with art if the leader is working right along with the group. Value each person's contribution, making a real effort to listen to what a person is saying through art.

Other Ways To Use *Growing Together*

We suggest sharing *Growing Together* with catechists, who may want to use some of its activities in age-graded religious education settings. Catechists will also appreciate the chapter introductions, which provide concise summaries of seasons and feasts, and the bibliography of valuable resources for religious educators.

Building a Parish Family

Introduction and Information

Fall is the time when many parishes gather together again after summer vacation. It's a good time to explore what membership in the family of God bestows on us and requires of us.

Our membership begins at baptism, our full initiation by water and the Holy Spirit into the Church, the Body of Christ. The bond that God establishes with us at baptism lasts forever and cannot be broken.

Baptism also forges our bond with other members of the Church. This bond unites us despite all such distinctions as race, sex, culture and even age. Our children are as much members of the Body of Christ as we are.

The ancient and dramatic baptismal rite of the Church, designed for adult converts, made these bonds unforgettable. Three years of instruction and preparation culminated in days of fasting and prayer. At dawn, after an all-night vigil, the converts were plunged naked into running water as they affirmed the faith. They were clothed in robes, then brought into the Church for the kiss of peace from their new family.

A New Way of Life

Even children who had been baptized as infants could see by the annual re-enactment of the initiation of converts that to be a member of God's family was to be committed to a radically new way of life.

This understanding did not always survive the transformation of baptism from the central liturgy of the Church to a private ceremony for parents and godparents. Private celebrations shifted the emphasis from God's family to the nuclear family.

Now that baptism has been restored as a public rite of the Church, celebrated in the context of the Sunday Eucharist or at other feasts, children can once more begin to witness something of the mystery of God's adoption, enacted in baptism.

In the rite of baptism for children, the celebrant and the congregation affirm the renunciation of sin and profession of faith made by the parents and godparents on behalf of those to be baptized. Our profession incorporates the Apostles' Creed, our affirmation of whole-hearted trust in God the Father, Son and Holy Spirit. The children are baptized, then anointed with chrism as the celebrant proclaims their anointing by Christ and their incorporation into the body of he who was anointed Priest, Prophet and King.

Growing Together

Our Priestly, Prophetic and Kingly Calling

We share in Christ's anointing and calling both. The documents of Vatican II and the *Catechism of the Catholic Church* (#901-#913) both proclaim that the laity share in the priestly, prophetic and kingly offices of Christ through their worship, witness and wisdom in ordering their daily lives.

What implications does this calling have for our parish families?

Members of God's family are to find nourishment in the Church's teaching, its offer of companionship, its sacraments (especially the Eucharist) and its intimacy with God through prayer.

Members of God's family find their value, not in worldly achievement, but in servanthood. In the poor, we see Christ. In the diseased, we see Christ. In the "impossible" child, we see Christ. In the lost and lonely, we see Christ. In the enemy (within and without), we see Christ. We believe in our power, through the Holy Spirit, to heal those who are broken in body or spirit and to feed those who are hungry.

Members of God's family share God's love of diversity in the human family, recognizing that all of its members are God's children, created in God's image. We fully believe that only in God can we find safety and that our only strength is love. We revere the mystery of life and seek ways to preserve its chalice, the earth.

Members of God's family are called to recognize all that is hurtful and destructive within ourselves and the world in which we live. We are called to perfect wholeness. Even when we miss the mark, we are never to despair of God's forgiveness or God's power to transform us into "a new creation."

Members of God's family are to live as Jesus did, proclaiming the unfailing, all-encompassing love of God, both by word and way of life. This is a Love that, when battered to death by human hatred, was unwilling even then to give up on us. This is a Love that resurrected itself in the greatest moment of all time, to return to us and never leave. Good news: The kingdom of God is at hand!

Renewing Ourselves, Renewing Our Parish Family

With the end of summer's lazy days, many of us—adults and children—feel renewed in purpose and energy. Now is the time, in a parish family session, to examine our baptismal calling. To what does God call us? How can we support one another in answering God's call? Seeking answers to these questions together can draw us closer to each other and to God, renewing us as a true family.

Help! How do I plan this session?

How will I publicize this session?

_____

_____

How many people do I think might participate? _____

What are the ages of the participants?

_____

Where will we hold the session?

_____

Which recommended activities would work best with this particular group of participants? (Remember, we provide more activities than most groups can use in a single session. Pick a few that will work for your group.)

_____

_____

_____

_____

_____

_____

_____

Volunteers

to do	names	phone numbers
planning:		
preparation and set-up:		
activity leaders:		
clean-up:		

Growing Together

Session Plan

Gathering Prayer

Use the "Blessing for a Family or Household" from *Catholic Household Blessings and Prayers*, p. 206-210 or proclaim one of the lectionary readings for the week.

Key Idea

Members of God's family share in Christ's priestly office as they come together, week by week, to worship together, bringing the sacrifices of their daily life and prayer to the celebration of the Eucharist.

Small Group Activity: Murals of the Early Church and Our Parish

Materials

Bible
masking tape
roll of newsprint or butcher paper
scissors
felt markers

Optional:
other drawing materials such as crayons, chalks, pastels, etc.

Ask someone to read Acts 2:42-47, a description of life in the early Christian community. Ask the group to divide into two groups to make two murals, one depicting life in the first church family, and one depicting life in your own parish family.

Ask the latter group to include ways that the parish carries out its baptismal calling to community, to Eucharist and to prayer. Make certain that children know the meaning of the word *apostles* (the first followers of Jesus).

Tape two strips of newsprint to the wall at a height appropriate for children as well as adults. Allow at least one foot in length for each person drawing.

When the murals are finished, encourage an informal discussion with these questions:
● What do you see in this mural? (Ask this question twice, once for each mural.)

 ## Leader's Tip

 Encourage reluctant drawers to use stick figures and similar simple techniques. A leader who is not skilled in art, and who will draw quickly and simply, can act as a model for those embarrassed about their drawing skills.

- What things do you see in both murals? What things appear only in the mural of the first church family? What things appear only in the mural of our own parish family?
- Why do you think the two murals show different things?
- What do you like best about each mural?

Good discussions respect, and seek to fulfill, the needs of all the participants.

Leader's Tip

Do not try to aim a parish family discussion at the very youngest participants. Instead, try to ask open-ended questions, i.e., What do you think? What do you feel? Such questions allow all ages to respond. Be aware of different needs of the various age levels when they answer.

 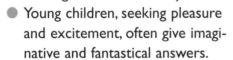

- Young children, seeking pleasure and excitement, often give imaginative and fantastical answers.
- Older primary and intermediate children, seeking approval, often give whatever answers the questioner seems to want.
- Teenagers, seeking to hide their identity struggles, may not want to answer at all, lest anyone in the group disagree.
- Some adults, seeking to reconcile new information with an orderly world view, may give systematic and logical answers.
- 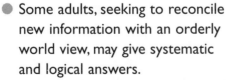Some adults, seeking to explore ambiguities, may answer with another question!

Small Group Activity: Three Kinds of Prayer

Materials

newsprint
felt markers and crayons
long sheet of shelf paper

Break into three groups. Give each group a different assignment. Ask the groups each to work collectively to produce one prayer. (If your parish family is very large, you may want to break into more groups, giving several groups the same assignment.)

Provide the first group with newsprint and markers. Invite the group to write a prayer that is an acrostic. Ask participants to base the acrostic on the word **church**, and to write a prayer asking God to bless the parish church in particular ways. To write the acrostic, spell out the word **church** vertically. Let each letter of the word begin a line of your prayer.

For example:
C all your people together, O God.
H elp us to love and serve you.
U se our church home as a home to all.
R enew our spirits with your Holy Spirit.
C are for the poor through us.
H elp us always to rejoice in your love.

Ask younger members to draw a decorative border around the prayer.

Ask the second group to compose new words to a familiar, popular tune (not a hymn). The new words are to offer praise to God. Be sure that children understand

Growing Together

that *praise* means to say in various ways, "We love you, God."

Give the third group a long sheet of shelf paper and felt markers or crayons. Ask each member to draw something on the paper for which he or she is thankful. Words may also be added.

Take time to reconvene the entire group to share what each group has created. The leader may want to point out that the first group's prayer is a petition, that is, it asks God for something. The second group's prayer offers praise, expressing love for God. The third group's prayer thanks God for blessings. Any of us can pray in any of these ways any time.

Small Group Activity: Helping Hand Cut-Outs

Materials

    9"x 12" construction paper, various
        colors, 1 sheet per participant
    felt pens
    clear tape
    scissors

Give each participant a piece of construction paper, scissors and a felt pen. Ask each participant to draw around his or her hands and then cut out the two drawings.

Directions to participants: On one cut-out write a way that you sought out God or served Christ this past week. On the other cut-out write a way that you will seek out God or serve Christ this week. Adults

should write for any children too young to write.

Then ask all participants to tape the cut-outs together to make a long string of helping hands. Post the string in your meeting room or in a long hallway.

Small Group Activity: Balloons and Pennants

Materials

    balloons
    ribbon
    clear tape
    scissors
    12" x 18" construction paper
    glue
    felt markers

Ask the group to brainstorm rules that we must live by. If discussion is slow, suggest that we have traffic rules, school rules, rules in our work places and rules for games. Explain that the Bible gives us two rules that are more important to God than all the other rules we must follow.

Break into smaller groups. Ask each group to look up Matthew 22:36-40. Discuss:
● What are the two most important rules?

- Why are these rules more important than any others?
- Is it Christian to love ourselves? How can we show love for ourselves?

If we love others as we love ourselves, how will we treat others? How will we express anger to others? How will we respond when someone hurts us? How can we show people we love them?

Provide each group with a piece of construction paper, scissors, glue, balloons, ribbon, clear tape and a felt marker. Ask each group to make a pennant that proclaims the two most important rules and to decorate the pennant with a bunch of balloons. (You may want to provide the kind of narrow ribbon that curls when pulled tightly over a scissors blade.)

Encourage diversity and creative thinking. Ask each group to make its banner as festive as possible. Donate these pennants to the religious education program, so that the pennants can decorate classrooms.

Large Group Activity: Name Tags

Materials

    construction paper
    scissors
    glue
    felt pens
    crayons
    masking tape

This activity helps the members of your parish family become better acquainted and more aware of each member's uniqueness. Ask each participant to find a partner, encouraging older participants to pair with younger ones. Ask each pair to find out as much as possible about each other, then make name tags for each other.

Growing Together

Useful questions can include:
- What do you like to eat?
- What is your favorite color? Why?
- What games do you like?
- What's your favorite part of the day?
- What work do you like to do?
- What animals do you like?
- What's your favorite song?

Each name tag should convey as much as possible about the person for whom it is made. After everyone has a name tag (stick on with a masking tape loop), serve punch and cookies and ask people to circulate to read each other's tags.

Key Idea

Members of God's family share in Christ's prophetic office as they struggle against "this present darkness, against the spiritual hosts of wickedness." By their daily lives, they proclaim the gospel and serve others in Christ.

In this section, the first three activities are based on Bible stories of repentance. The stories tell of Zacchaeus, the tax collector who made amends for his wily ways, the parable of the lost coin and the parable of the lost sheep.

The two parables compare people who have found something that was lost with the hosts of heaven who rejoice when one sinner repents. All three stories indicate the true meaning of repentance, which is not only saying "I'm sorry," but undergoing a deep change of heart and behavior. Repentance means seeking and once again being found by God.

If you choose to use one of these activities as a presentation to your whole parish family, remember to ask the audience: What is the connection between the Bible story and our baptismal calling to continual repentance?

Small Group Activity: Make-Believe "Slide Show"

Materials

Bibles or copies of Luke 19:1-10

Ask a small group to produce a make-believe slide show of the story of Zacchaeus. The group first reads the story and decides who will play the parts of the narrator, Jesus, Zacchaeus, and the crowd.

Then the group decides how to portray each scene in the story by posing the characters as though for a photograph. They pose without moving and over-dramatize facial expressions and stance to convey the drama of the scene.

For example, in the first scene, Zacchaeus might be standing on tip-toe, trying to see over the crowd hanging on to Jesus. Once the scenes are chosen, the group practices

20

with the narrator, who reads the story from a Good News Bible as the group poses for each scene.

The narrator tells the people in the audience to close their eyes while the "slide show" is made ready. (The group poses to portray the first scene.) When the narrator says "click," the people in the audience open their eyes and hear the narrator recount the first part of the story. Continue through the story in this fashion.

Small Group Activity: Find the Lost Coin (game)

Materials

Bibles or copies of Luke 15:8-10
a "gold" coin made of cardboard, covered with metallic gift wrap

In the parable of the lost coin, Jesus tells us that, like a woman who rejoices over finding a coin she has lost, the angels rejoice over the sinner who repents. **Before the session** hide the coin in your meeting room (or if weather permits, outdoors).

In the session ask the group assigned this activity to read the passage, then to go looking for the coin. Hunt in pairs, making sure that each young child is paired with an older person. When the coin is found the rest of the group can make up a cheer, rejoicing over the coin that is found. (Later this group can share the cheer with the rest of your parish family.)

Small Group Activity: Melodrama

Materials

Bibles
12" x 18" construction paper
markers

Ask the group to read Luke 15:4-7, the parable of the lost sheep. Here Jesus tells us that all of heaven rejoices when a sinner repents, like a shepherd who has found a lost sheep.

Next have the group make cue cards for the audience. Print in large letters each of these words or phrases on a sheet of construction paper:
● Cheer and clap!
● Boo and hiss!
● Thanks be to God!

Ask a member of the group to narrate the story. Other members of the group can play the parts of the shepherd, the lost sheep, the other 99 sheep and a person to hold up the cue cards.

The narrator recounts the story, inviting the members playing Jesus and the lost sheep to improvise their own dialogue. The lost sheep might be a child who scampers all around the room (and amongst the audience) pretending to explore trees, rocks and streams.

Use the cue cards to tell the audience how to respond at various points in the story. Save the cue card that reads "Thanks be to God" for the end of the story.

Growing Together

Small Group Activity: Repentance Roleplay

Materials

chalkboard or newsprint

Ask each participant to imagine that he or she has just hurt a close friend or family member. Ask the group to brainstorm actions that could be taken next. Record all suggestions on chalkboard or newsprint.

Divide the group into pairs. Ask each pair to roleplay one of the actions suggested. Ask one member of the pair to play the person who did the hurtful action and the other member of the pair to play the person who was hurt. Each roleplay begins with the person who was hurt saying, "What you just did (or said) really hurt!"

When all the pairs are finished, discuss:

- How did the people who were pretending to have hurt a friend feel when the friend said, "What you just did really hurt"?
- How did the people who were pretending to have been hurt feel about stating their feelings so directly? How do you respond to hurts in most situations? Is saying you are hurt a good thing to do? Why or why not?
- Which of the ways that were suggested to handle the situation do you like best? Why?

Vote on the five best ways to handle the situation and report these to the rest of your parish family.

Small Group Activity: Rainbow Sign of Good News

Materials

colored chalk
4' sheet of white butcher paper
felt markers
masking tape
Bibles
prepared slips of paper in basket

Divide into 10 groups. Ask one group to make a large sign picturing a rainbow by taping the butcher paper to a smooth wall and drawing with colored chalk. The rainbow needs to fill the entire sheet and include nine stripes.

Before the session write the scripture references below on slips of paper and put them in a basket. In the session pass the basket to the other nine groups and have each group draw one slip.

Here are the references to write on the slips of paper. Number each slip. *The information identifying each passage is for the leader of your session; do not include it on the slips:*

1. Mark 4:35-39   Jesus calms a storm.

2. Mark 6:34-44   Jesus feeds 5,000.

3. Mark 6:54-56   Jesus heals many.

4. Mark 10:13-16   Jesus blesses children.

5. Mark 16:1-7   Jesus is risen!

6. John 3:16-17   Jesus came to save us.

7. John 14:15-17   Jesus promises that the Holy Spirit will come.

8. Acts 2:1-4   The Holy Spirit comes to fill believers.

9. John 15:9-17   Jesus loves us; we who follow him bear fruit and are filled with joy.

Ask each group to look up its passage and to compose one sentence that tells the good news that the passage announces to us. Ask each group to compose its sentence in the present tense. For example: The good news in the story of Noah and the ark is that God promises never to destroy the world again.

MAKE 9 BANDS IN RAINBOW

WRITE THE GOOD NEWS ON EACH BAND

Ask each group to send someone to the rainbow to write the group's sentence on one of the colored stripes. Make group #1's stripe the lowest one. Each group adds its sentence in numerical order. The very top stripe announces Jesus' love for us and our joy.

After all the groups are finished, reconvene and ask each group to tell which story the group read and what good news the story has for us.

Large Group Activity: Sidewalk Art

Materials

> sidewalk outside your building
> colored chalk
> prepared slips of paper in basket
> Bibles

Before the session write on a separate slip of paper each one of the Bible passages listed in the Rainbow Sign Activity above.

At the session invite participants to consider ways we proclaim God's good news. Divide into nine groups and ask each group to draw a slip of paper. Ask each group to read its passage, then go outdoors and use colored chalk to write and draw on the sidewalk the good news announced by the group's passage. Encourage multi-colored lettering and pictures that tell the story or message of each passage.

Take time to wander around and see each other's work. The first good rain will wash away your sidewalk art, but you will have proclaimed the good news to your community with color and creativity.

Growing Together

▶ **Large Group Activity:**
TV News Interviews

Materials

prepared slips of paper in basket

Before the session write on a separate slip of paper each one of the Bible passages listed in the Rainbow Sign Activity above.

In your session divide into nine groups and ask each group to draw a slip of paper. Each group reads its passage and then comes up with a mock TV news interview. The group chooses a member to play the part of an eyewitness who saw the event described in the group's Bible passage or heard Jesus say the words of the passage.

The other members are to play reporters who question the eyewitness about what has just happened that has sparked rumors of good news all over the countryside. The reporters should try to get as many details about the story from the eyewitness as possible.

Reconvene and present the interviews to the entire group. Or if you are short of time, ask each group to tell what good news was announced by its passage.

Note: For a more ambitious project, turn this into a video-taped activity.

▶ **Small Group Activity:**
Story Telling

Materials

Optional:
large sheets of newsprint
felt markers; thick, child-sized crayons;
or colored chalk

Here is a less structured activity that allows participants to tell their own Bible stories. Seat everyone in a circle. Ask each participant to think of a favorite story about Jesus. Ask volunteers to tell their stories as briefly and dramatically as possible. Continue for as much time as you have allotted for this activity.

You may prefer to ask each participant to draw a picture of his or her favorite story first. Participants can then use their pictures to tell the stories.

Note: This is an especially effective parish family activity if older participants are encouraged to treat the stories of younger participants with deep respect.

▶ **Small Group Activity:**
Going On a Journey (game)

Materials

Bible

Seat participants in a circle. Read, or tell in your own words, the story of Jesus' instructions to the disciples, Luke 9:1-6.

Begin the game by saying, "I am going on a journey to tell God's Good News, and I *don't* need (*name an object*)." Ask the next participant to repeat this sentence, naming your object first, then adding a new object.

Continue around your circle, encouraging humorous and farfetched responses. If the list breaks down, simply begin a new list with the next participant.

Modify this game for younger participants, if necessary, by eliminating the repetitions.

Small Group Activity: Guessing the Good News

Materials

Bibles

Ask a small group to prepare to present Matthew 11:2-6 in mime to the entire group. A narrator can begin by reading aloud verses 2-4. Ask the audience, without reading the passage, to guess what good news is being mimed by the small group.

Note: The good news is that "The blind receive their sight and the lame walk, lepers are cleansed and the deaf hear, and the dead are raised up, and the poor have good news preached to them." (Mt. 11:5)

Leader's Resources: Outreach

- Follow up activities that encourage participation in parish outreach or social justice programs with practical information participants can use. Consider providing information about the next food or clothing drive, or dates and times for families to help out at the soup kitchen or homeless shelter.
- Any of the prayers for peace and justice that are included in the Roman Catholic *Sacramentary,* "Masses and Prayers for Various Needs and Occasions," #22, p. 902, could be used in these activities.

Key Idea

Members of God's family share in Christ's kingly office as they work for justice and peace. Through their daily ministry, they promote God's kingdom of love and mercy, welcoming God's riches of human diversity.

Growing Together

▶ Large Group Activity: Parish Fair

Materials

    36" roll of butcher paper
    felt marker
    scissors
    masking tape
    pens or pencils

Before the session contact the leadership of every group or ministry in your parish to organize a Parish Fair. Ask each group to prepare a display that invites participants to sign up for that group. Suggested displays:

- Catechists might prepare one activity—such as a relay race or a mural—in which learners can participate as they sign up for fall classes.
- Music groups might lead a contemporary hymn sing in one corner of the room.
- Service groups might present snapshot pictures of ministry carried out in the previous year. These groups also might invite participants to sign petitions or write letters to government officials about such issues as the homeless and hungry in your community. (Provide names and addresses of officials, paper, pens and envelopes.) This group might also hold a bread baking session to make bread for the poor.
- Parish groups might present a colorful calendar of projected activities and invite participants to play get-acquainted games.

Such a group might also provide materials to make name tags. Ask each person to write his or her name vertically on a name tag. Then fill in a personal quality, gift, talent or interest next to each letter. The word written next to each letter should begin with that letter.

For example:
M akes photographs as hobby
A lways on time
R eads mysteries
I s a teacher
A rtistic

Use butcher paper to prepare a life-sized silhouette figure of Jesus. Use a felt marker to divide the torso, upper arms and thighs into as many segments as there are groups participating in the Parish Fair.

Cut along the lines to separate the segments. Give one segment to each group to label with the group's name.

Either have participants sign up for activities directly on the segments, reassembling the figure at the end of the session, *or* reassemble the figure before the session and use as a graphic display—the Body of Christ in your parish—for the Parish Fair.

Building a Parish Family

Small Group Activity: The Great Commandment Relay Race

Materials

    3" x 5" cards
    felt marker
    Bible

Before the session write the words of the great commandment on 3" x 5" cards by writing a separate word on each card. The commandment is: "Love the Lord your God with all your heart, and with all your soul, and with all your mind and with all your strength...love your neighbor as yourself" (from Mk. 12:30-31).

Run this relay race while other activities are going on. Invite two teams of 10 or 12 people each to play at a time.

Line up the two teams at a starting line. About 15 feet away at the finish line place the two stacks of cards, one stack in front of each group. Scramble each team's cards and tell the players that when their team's cards are put in correct order, the cards will reveal a "secret message."

When the leader says "go," each team sends a runner to pick up one of the cards in that team's stack and bring the card back to the team. Once the first runner reaches the team, a second runner is sent to get another card. Meanwhile the rest of the team tries to put the cards in order so that the team can figure out the secret message. The first team to put the cards in correct order wins.

Large Group Activity: Prayers for Peace

Materials

    old newspapers
    12" x 18" construction paper
    glue sticks or rubber cement
    felt pens or crayons
    masking tape or clothesline and spring-
       clip clothespins

Ask all participants to close their eyes and silently imagine the world at complete peace. No one is hurting anyone else. All God's children love each other. Allow a few seconds for this meditation.

Then ask participants to open their eyes and brainstorm the implications:
- What would happen to wars?
- What would we do with weapons?
- What would we do with prisons?
- How would we care for people who are poor and hungry?
- How would we use natural resources?

Ask the youngest children to draw pictures, using crayons or felt pens on construction paper, of how the world would look at complete peace.

Give each older participant a sheet of construction paper. Provide newspapers and glue sticks or rubber cement to share. Ask each older participant to create a prayer for peace by tearing letters, phrases or words from newspaper headlines and gluing these to the construction paper.

Tape the prayers and drawings to your wall or hang them on a clothesline for everyone to read.

Growing Together

Small Group Activity: Bible Reflections (for older participants)

Materials

Bibles

Ask the participants to close their eyes as you read a passage of scripture aloud. Explain that at a certain point in the story you will ask several questions, pausing after each question for a minute or two so that each participant can answer silently, as though the question is a personal one.

Read Matthew 25:31-40. Pause after verse 37, after verse 38 and after verse 39.

After this meditation, ask participants to open their eyes and discuss:

- How central are the kinds of good works mentioned in this passage to peace and justice?
- How central are such works to being a Christian? How can we be involved with helping the needy when we have families to support or other jobs to do?
- Do we benefit in some personal way here and now by helping people in need? How do our small acts of kindness cause a ripple effect?
- If we take a close look at our checkbooks, what does this tell us about how highly we value peace and justice?
- What are we doing personally to work for justice and peace?
- What is our parish doing to encourage peace and justice?

Leader's Resources: Multicultural Issues

- Precede or follow the session with a pot luck featuring ethnic foods brought by families in the group. These days, many different ethnic groups are represented in the typical Catholic parish: Hispanics from Central America, Asians from Viet Nam or the Philippines, African Americans, families descended from immigrants from Western "Catholic countries," such as Poland or Ireland or Italy, etcetera.
- Consider hosting a discussion or presentation about the ethnic origins of different participating families into each session. This might reinforce the "catholic" nature of Catholicism and of Catholic identity.

Closing Prayers

Choose one of these closing prayers:
- Form a large circle by holding hands. Ask for volunteers one by one to bring to the center of the circle each item created by the group today. As this happens, ask other volunteers to offer brief thanksgivings for some blessing that came from the activity represented by each object.

For example:

> "Thank you, God, for giving me joy
> as we danced together and sang that
> we are your people" or "Thank you,
> God, for my new friend who made a
> beautiful name tag for me."

- Ask everyone to sit comfortably on
  chairs or the floor. Invite participants to
  pray together the Our Father.

- Pray for the religious education program
  just beginning. Pray for those who will
  teach and those who will learn.

All Saints

Introduction and Information

On All Saints, November 1, we celebrate the communion of saints and recognize God's desire to sanctify the lives of all believers.

In any year, All Saints may be observed on the Sunday following November 1 in addition to its observance on the fixed date. If November 1 falls on Sunday, the lectionary readings for All Saints take precedence.

The Church, from its very beginning, understood the Body of Christ to encompass all baptized people, both the living and the dead. All are united in a mystical communion of saints by virtue of baptism (1 Cor. 6:11).

The Communion of Saints

In the Apostles' Creed we state our belief in "the communion of saints." There are at least three perspectives on the meaning of this phrase; for a more complete understanding, see *The Catechism of the Catholic Church*, #946-948.

From one perspective, it describes the spiritual union existing between each Christian and Christ. This union in Christ brings about the union of all Christians with one another, the living and the dead.

From another perspective, we take special joy in the common life we know with one another here on earth. From a third perspective, we rejoice in our common participation in the holy gifts of the sacraments, especially the Eucharist.

All these perspectives describe one holy mystery. Christians share a special union with one another, which is forged by the act of the Holy Spirit in baptism and strengthened by the work of the same Spirit in the Eucharist. This union is most visible among those Christians presently alive.

Yet, Christians do not exclude from this fellowship in Christ those who are dead. After death, the faithful departed are not severed from union in Christ. The apostle Paul forcefully states this conviction in Romans 8:38-39:

> *For I am sure that neither death, nor life, nor angels, nor principalities, nor things present, nor things to come, nor powers, nor height, nor depth, nor anything else in all creation, will be able to separate us from the love of God in Christ Jesus our Lord.*

How All Saints Came to Be

From the beginning, the early Church especially honored martyrs, those who had died for their faith. Local churches kept a record of their local martyrs and each year

Growing Together

celebrated their "birthdays," the dates of their martyrdom.

By the fourth century many parts of the Church observed a day of commemoration for their martyrs, confessors (those who had been punished for their faith but did not die), and virgins, all of those known by name and unknown. In the East, the feast was, and still is, celebrated on the first Sunday after Pentecost. In the West it was celebrated during the Easter season, connecting the witness of the saints with Christ's victory over death.

As the Western Church spread into Northern Europe, it encountered pagan festivals held in late autumn to propitiate the evil spirits associated with the first killing frosts and the coming of winter, darkness and death. Our word *Halloween* originally meant All Hallows' (Saints') Eve.

To make a Christian response, the Church transferred the celebration of the saints to November 1 and called it All Saints. It then developed as a day of remembrance of the faithful departed, incorporating what had been called All Souls' Day (November 2).

Sanctity Through Baptism

Too often Christians have used the term *saint* to describe those of extraordinary sanctity. We need to remember that New Testament usage describes *all* Christians as saints. Paul uses this phrase to describe even the unruly Corinthians (1 Cor. 1:2)—saints by virtue of their baptism. Thus, our All Saints festivities should include a celebration of our own membership in the

communion of saints, the membership that began for each of us through the sacrament of baptism.

Ways to Celebrate

All Saints is one of the Holy Days of the Church. This feast—so important in the Church year, but often neglected by current custom—represents an ideal opportunity for a parish to devise its own ceremonies and celebrations.

One parish celebrates this feast with a procession of banners, accompanied by a brass quartet. Another parish invites members of a local symphony orchestra to provide music for a Mozart mass, followed by an elegant luncheon. Several parishes hold Saints' day parties, encouraging children to come dressed as saints from the Bible or saints from more recent history.

Our celebration is enhanced by the awareness of our fellowship with those saints departed. Not even death can sever the relationship that the faithful have in Christ.

Our Vocation as Saints

Some saints—such as Francis of Assisi or Teresa of Avila—have inspired affectionate recollection over the centuries. Other saints have left not even their names to Christian posterity.

Prominent or not, these saints who precede us in the Church's pilgrimage to God are the recipients of our special honor on All Saints. What we honor in these saints is God's own Spirit within them, leading them—as God leads us—to sanctity. This is the highest aspect of our celebration of All Saints day, the celebration of the vocation of every Christian to be a saint, a holy one of God.

This vocation is manifest in Jesus' life and in his teaching, most especially in the Beatitudes. "Happy are those who know they are spiritually poor...who mourn... who are humble...whose greatest desire is to do what God requires...who are merciful...the pure in heart...who work for peace...who are persecuted because they do what God requires" (Mt. 5:3-10).

This costly vocation may bewilder many, who see in the Beatitudes not happiness but waste. Christians are often accused of being unrealistic and impractical, of following a first century rabbi—perhaps kindly, certainly deluded—whose death was a defeat and whose resurrection was a myth.

So be it. We know whom we have believed; we know for whose kingdom we long. Let all the faithful rejoice in triumph on All Saints—we are one with the Lord and God's holy ones. Alleluia!

Growing Together

Help! How do I plan this session?

How will I publicize this session?

_____

_____

How many people do I think might participate? _____

What are the ages of the participants?

_____

Where will we hold the session?

_____

Which recommended activities would work best with this particular group of participants? (Remember, we provide more activities than most groups can use in a single session. Pick a few that will work for your group.)

_____

_____

_____

_____

_____

_____

_____

_____

Volunteers

to do	names	phone numbers
planning:		
preparation and set-up:		
activity leaders:		
clean-up:		

Session Plan

Gathering Prayer

Begin the celebration with song: either a rousing chorus of "When the Saints Go Marching In," the Litany of the Saints or the Beatitudes.

Key Idea

All Saints, a Holy Day of the Church, is a time to honor past saints whose lives have radiated the love of God to all the world. Special ceremony and celebration are appropriate to this day.

Large Group Activity: All Saints' Party

Materials

decorations
refreshments
Optional:
plain, large sugar cookies
tubes of icing

Invite the parish family to a Saints Party. Invite everyone to come dressed as a biblical saint or a saint from more recent history.

If desired, include plain cookies as part of the refreshments. Encourage participants to decorate the cookies with the symbols of various saints, using the tubes of icing. You will find a list of symbols for some unfamiliar saints on page 43.

To make the party informative as well as fun, choose other activities from this chapter. You may also want to tell the following story as part of the entertainment.

Story: Why Do We Celebrate Today?

Long, long ago, the people who lived in what we now call England and France were known as Celts. (You can say *selts* or *kelts*.) They had no electric lights, freezers to store food, or central heating. The Celts worried that the cold, dark winter would bring hunger, sickness and sometimes even death.

The Celts had another reason to fear winter. They believed that it was the season when witches and evil ghosts flew everywhere. The Celts even believed that ghosts slipped inside animals who roamed around playing tricks on everyone.

Growing Together

To scare away the ghosts, the Celts lighted big bonfires. They did magic and wore costumes to fool the evil ghosts into thinking that the Celts themselves were ghosts.

When Christians (people who believe in Christ) came to the land of the Celts, the Christians told everyone some good news: All of us who follow Jesus are saints. When we die, we don't turn into scary ghosts. We go to live happily with God. Even our bodies are made new again in a real way, just as Jesus' body was made new on the first Easter Day.

Long ago the Christians in England chose a special day to honor all the saints, or followers of Jesus, who had died. November 1 was chosen as All Hallows' Day, which we now call All Saints. The evening before was called All Hallows' Eve, which we now call Halloween.

Even after Christians told the good news, however, some people still wore frightening costumes and burned bonfires to scare away evil ghosts. For hundreds of years, many people have continued as the Celts did, to practice witchcraft, fortune telling and magic charms.

Christians know, however, that there is a power far mightier than any of these practices: the power of prayer. Praying to God is more powerful than the biggest bonfire to overcome any evil!

Large Group Activity: Interviews

Materials

> costumes
> chairs
> *Optional:*
> long table

Before the session ask several participants to roleplay saints at the All Saints session. Either see the bibliography for reference books that the participants can use to learn saints' stories or have the participants pick biblical saints only. Ask these participants to devise appropriate costumes.

At the session, you can provide a separate area to seat each "saint," or you can seat all the "saints" together as a panel at a long table.

Invite other participants to interview these "saints." Those participants roleplaying saints should be as prepared to answer "When were you born?" as "Do you like spaghetti?"

Learning Centers

To teach the lives of various saints, set up learning centers in corners of a large room or in separate small rooms. At each center, tell a story of a saint and invite participants to join in an activity that complements the story. Stories and activities follow.

Story:
Mary, Mother of Jesus

(This is an especially good story if the session includes very young children. Stop to talk over the questions with participants, especially encouraging children to answer.)

Do you remember when Jesus was born? Do you remember the name of that special day? What a beautiful day that is for us! Do you remember the name of Jesus' mother?

That's right! Her name was Mary. We also call her the Blessed Virgin Mary. What are some of the things we remember about her?

She lived when there were no cars. How do you think she and her family got around? She lived when there were no supermarkets where she could buy her bread or food. How do you think she and her family made food to eat? She lived when there were no department stores to buy her clothes. How do you think she and her family made clothes to wear? Like all men and women of her day, Mary worked hard.

But her most important work was to say "Yes!" to God when God asked Mary to do something special for all the people in the world. What did God ask Mary to do?

Mary said yes. Mary became the mother of Jesus. What do mothers do?

Well, Mary did these things for her son, Jesus, and she did them all with love. As a boy, Jesus learned about God's love from his mother Mary.

That is what saints do, you know. Saints want to become God's close friends. They do all the jobs God gives them the best that they can, with deep love in their hearts, and they ask God to help them.

This poem reminds us of what God could have said to Mary:

"Mary, Mary, strong and kind,
Gently rock this child of mine.
Care for him, and tell him too,
Of my love for all of you."

(While the poem is recited, children might enjoy rocking an imaginary baby in their arms.)

 ## Leader's Tip

 Several videos available from St. Anthony Messenger Press and Franciscan Communications (Cincinnati, OH; 1-800-488-0488) are perfect for Learning Centers for young children. We suggest:

 Saint Francis of Assisi
Heroes of the Faith
(These animated videos present such popular saints as Francis, Patrick, Francis Xavier, Bernadette and Nicholas.)

Growing Together

Small Group Activity: Flowers for Mary

Materials

bright colors of construction paper
yarn or green pipe cleaners
glue
facial tissues

Each participant may make one or more paper flowers, using one of the methods suggested:

- Pinch a paper tissue in the center and twist it several times. These can be formed into a lei by catching the twisted "stem" in a knot along a length of yarn. Or one flower can be attached to the clothes or to a paper headband. Or a pipe cleaner can be twisted onto the base of the flower to form a stem.
- For each flower, have three heart shapes cut from construction paper. Fold these vertically. Glue one side of each of two hearts to the third heart. Then glue the remaining halves together. Insert a pipe cleaner with a spot of glue on it at the points of the hearts to make stems.

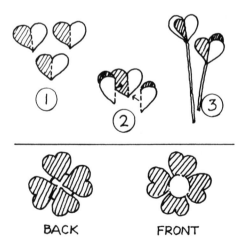

- Have four heart shapes and one circle cut from construction paper for each flower. The participant glues four hearts *by their points **only*** to the circle. Fold up the heart petals slightly. Attach to pipe cleaner or staple to bulletin board above a drawn-on green stem and leaves.

Story: Saint Lucia Tells Her Story

(The storyteller may want to dress as Swedish girls do on St. Lucia's Day. A long white dress, red sash and a crown of greenery with candles in it are appropriate. Set the crown on a table and let older children use a taper to light the candles.)

My name is St. Lucia. I lived more than fifteen hundred years ago, across the ocean in Italy. The people of my country still tell of a long-ago famine, when some people had so little to eat that they were starving. They became weak and sick with worry.

The people with no food knew that I cared about feeding poor, hungry people, so they came to me for help. Can you guess what I did to help? I did the very thing you can do when you need help. I prayed and asked God for food, and I asked all the hungry people to pray with me.

While we prayed, a ship sailed into our harbor carrying a boatload of wheat. My people were saved! We shouted and cheered and thanked God for answering our prayers. And we cooked the wheat and had plenty to eat.

A holiday in my honor is celebrated on December 13. In Sweden where the sun only shines a few hours a day in midwinter, the children have a saying: "Lucy-light, the shortest day and the longest night."

Old people in some parts of Sweden say that at dawn on St. Lucia's Day you might glimpse me crossing a frozen lake, carrying food to the poor. Now that is only a story; you won't really see me, but you might indeed see girls and boys dressed in white going from house to house.

The girls carry candles and one of them dresses as Saint Lucia, wearing a white dress and a red sash, with candles in her hair. The children visit each house in their village to serve sweet Lucia buns, which are similar to cinnamon buns, and steaming coffee. And that's what we're going to do now...

Small Group Activity: Making Lucia Buns

Use a conventional or toaster oven to bake refrigerator cinnamon buns in class. Or, using a recipe from any Swedish-American cookbook, make dough for Lucia buns **before the session**, and invite the participants to shape the rolls and bake them.

Story: Saint Francis and the Wolf

(You can use sack puppets for visual reinforcement. You might decorate the wolf puppet with fake fur.)

Saint Francis was a man who loved God and was a special friend to the animals, plants and people in God's world. Saint Francis often thanked God for giving us the sun to keep us warm and the moon to help us see at night. This good priest thanked God for making cool winds blow and for giving us fire and water.

One day Francis took a walk through the countryside near his home. As he came back to town, the townspeople came rushing out to meet him. They said in fearful voices, "Francis, Francis! A great gray wolf is killing our sheep! The wolf even growls at us and shows his sharp teeth. We're afraid! Please help us, Francis."

"A great gray wolf?" said Francis. "A wolf who kills sheep and growls? What else does this wolf do?"

More townspeople answered, telling Saint Francis other tales about the terrible wolf and his fierce ways. So Francis, who was a friend to all animals, said, "I'll go into the forest and speak to this wolf myself."

The people tried to stop Francis, saying, "But Francis, this wolf is truly fierce. He might hurt you."

Francis had made up his mind, though. First he knelt down to ask God to take care of him. Francis also said a prayer for the great gray wolf, then set off through the woods to find the animal.

It wasn't long before Francis saw the wolf sitting under a tree. Unafraid, Francis went right up to the great gray beast and said, "You shouldn't frighten or hurt the towns-people and their sheep because they, too, are God's creatures."

The wolf, no longer growling and looking fierce, stood there looking at St. Francis. St. Francis reached out gently and patted the wolf's head and scratched him behind the ears. The wolf put his huge head in St. Francis' lap.

From the edge of town the people saw the wolf with his head in St. Francis' lap. One by one they came up to the wolf and scratched behind his ears or gently patted his head.

Small Group Activity: Rhythm Band Orchestration

Materials

rhythm instruments for each element mentioned:
sun–cymbal
moon–finger cymbals
wind–vocal wind sounds
water–jingle bells or pouring water back and forth between two glasses
fire–rattle crumpled paper; add rhythm sticks or wood block sounds at random for the popping sounds of fire
earth–sand paper blocks

Explain that you are going to read a prayer written by Saint Francis. (This prayer is an adaptation of his *Ode to the Sun*.)

O good Lord God: Praise you! I love you.
Thank you for our brother, the sun.
Thank you for our sister, the moon.
Praise you for our brother, the wind.
Bless you for our sister, the water.
Praise you for our brother, the fire,
And for our mother, the earth.
Bless you, Lord, and thank you.

Distribute rhythm band instruments and assign each participant a part of creation. Instruct each participant to play his or her instrument at the mention of this part of creation.

Story: Saint Nicholas, Giver of Gifts

Just before Christmas, do you ever think of Santa's elves scurrying to wrap the very gifts that will soon appear under your tree? Have you ever wondered how Santa Claus came to be?

The real Santa Claus would have wanted us to celebrate Christmas first as Jesus' birthday and second as a time to give gifts. The real Santa Claus was named Saint Nicholas. In the fourth century, he became a bishop in a place called Myra, which is now the country of Turkey.

Legend has it that St. Nicholas once se-cretly gave three poor girls three sacks of gold. He is said to have saved three sailors from the stormy sea.

He stood firmly in his beliefs even when his faith got him in trouble; the government finally put him in jail. After he died, stories about him spread all over the world.

Centuries later Dutch children celebrated a special feast day in his honor, awaiting his secret arrival on a galloping, white horse.

For the horse, the children tucked hay and carrots into their shoes, hoping that St. Nicholas would leave toys and candy.

Stories say that this man of God was tall and lean. Pictures show him in his high hat (called a miter) and red robes. Today we can remember St. Nicholas by giving gifts to the poor and to each other in secret.

▶ Small Group Activity: Candy-Filled Miters

Materials

> red felt or construction paper
> gold braid or gold sequins
> glue
> red yarn
> hole punch
> candy canes

Even preschoolers (with help) can make small miters like the one St. Nicholas wore. Use the pattern provided here to cut out two small pieces of red felt or construction paper shaped like a miter for each participant. Punch holes along the sides of the two pieces. Give each participant red yarn to string through the holes to stitch the back and front of the miter

together. Decorate by gluing on gold braid or gold sequins in the shape of a cross. Tuck a candy cane or two in each miter.

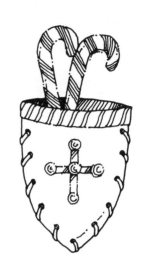

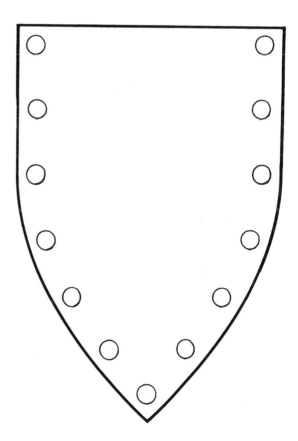

Growing Together

Small Group Activity: Banners, Pennants, Shields

In the pages that follow, you will find instructions for making banners, pennants and shields that commemorate saints. Choose from the list of materials, depending on which projects the group will do.

Materials

scissors
hole punch
string or twine
staples/staple gun
glue, tape
broomsticks or 1" doweling
heavy tape
flexible wire
screw eyes
ruler
hand saw
construction paper
cardboard
felt scraps
fabric scraps
aluminum foil
paint
glitter
sequins
paper strips
crayons
markers
sea shells
jingle bells
yarn
ribbon
crepe paper
tissue paper in various colors

Symbols for Saints

Traditional symbols for the saints can be found in reference books listed in the bibliography. Suggested symbols for biblical saints are:

Abraham: stars
Sarah: bread
Isaac: ram
Rebecca: water jar
Jacob: ladder
Leah: gazelle
Rachel: sheep
Moses: staff
Miriam: tambourine
Joseph: carpenter's tools
Mary: flower
Peter: rock or crossed keys
James and John: cups
Mary Magdalene: flask of oil (This symbol represents her healing. Mary Magdalene is not the woman who anointed the feet of Jesus before his death.)

General Suggestions for All Banners

- Use designs, words, names, suggested symbols, etc., for decorations.
- When banners are free-standing, decorate both sides.
- When possible, weight the bottom of cloth or paper banners.
- Reinforce the top of banners whenever possible. Yardsticks, dowels, wire rods, folded paper, or cardboard can be used. Reinforce holes with tape if using paper or thin fabric.

- Make notations on the backs of the banners giving the participants' names, the date and the parish name.

- Store banners in plastic bags. Leave the bottom of the bag open to allow air to circulate.

**St. Mary,
the Mother of Jesus**

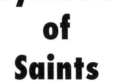

St. Lucia

St. Francis

St. Nicholas

St. Matthew

St. Mark

St. Luke

St. John

Growing Together

Crown Banner

Materials (additional)
round, gallon ice cream carton, or 36" x 15" strip of cloth or heavy paper
pole

Choose from two methods. Either form a circle with the cloth or paper strip, reinforcing the circular shape of the crown with a wire or cardboard hoop fastened to the lower inside edge. Or use a round ice cream carton, cutting away its bottom and covering it with paper.

Having used either method, now make the points of the crown by cutting large triangular notches. Punch holes at regular intervals around the base of the crown.

Ask the participants to decorate it with glitter, crayons, or markers. Participants can also tie or glue ribbon, yarn, or paper strips from the holes. Bells or sea shells can be added, as well.

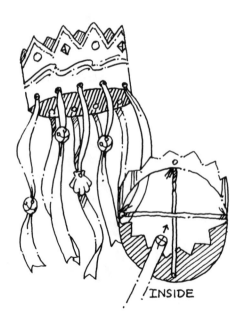

/ INSIDE

Punch holes in four points in the crown, opposite each other. Reinforce the holes and tie string or twine through them to create a hanger. Either notch the top of a pole with two perpendicular saw cuts, insert a screw eye in the end, or secure the crown with heavy tape.

Long Cylinder Banner

Materials (additional)
48" x 36" sheet of paper or fabric
6 36" x 5" strips of construction paper or fabric
pole
36" pieces of flexible wire or cardboard strips

Start by having the participants decorate the six 36" x 5" strips with symbols, names, or short phrases. These can be cut from paper, aluminum foil, felt, or fabric scraps. Position and mount the finished strips on the large sheet of paper or fabric with glue. Then make the banner into a long cylinder.

Add cardboard or wire reinforcers to the top and bottom of the cylinder. To finish it, punch four evenly spread holes near the top edge of the banner and thread them with string or twine to create a hanger. Either notch the top of the pole or attach the thread through a screw eye. Secure the banner with heavy tape or glue.

Note: The length and diameter of this banner can be adjusted to make it shorter, longer, smaller, or larger, depending on the age and height of the children carrying it and available materials.

Shields

Materials (additional)

square pieces of cardboard, approximately 2' x 2'

1" wide elastic banding or cardboard strips

Optional:

2' wood strip

Shields can be cut into various shapes: square, rectangular, oval, rounded, or pointed on the bottom, etc. Once the shape is cut, cover the cardboard with foil, construction paper, paint, or fabric. Designs can be added using any materials available, but try to use reflective materials if possible.

Once a shield is decorated, turn it over and tape or staple two loops, either elastic banding or cardboard, to create arm straps. (Position these according to the children's height.) If the shield starts to bend, reinforce it by adding a flat wooden strip across the top or middle.

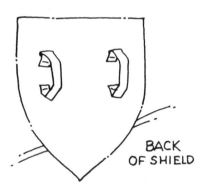

BACK OF SHIELD

Split Banners

Materials (additional)

2 12" x 24" strips of felt, other fabric, or paper

1 4-1/2' pole (notched on one end) and one 3' pole (notched on both ends)

Before the session make 12" x 24" panels of felt, other fabric, or paper. In the session help the participants decorate the panels. Designs or lettering can be drawn with markers or cut from available materials. Reflective materials will create a delightful eye-catcher.

To mount the panels, put them side by side, face down. Fold the top edge of each banner over the shorter pole and either tape, staple, or sew the edge to the panel. Do not attach the panels to the pole itself, rather let them slide and move.

Growing Together

Knot both ends of a 30" piece of wire or string and slide one knot into the notch on either end of the pole. Repeat at the other end with the second knot. Place the string into the notch of the larger pole and center the banner to balance it. Lash the two poles together with wire or twine to make them more secure.

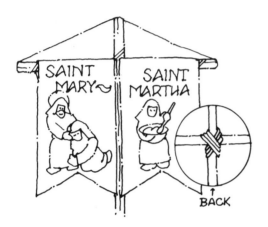

Pennants

Materials (additional)

12" x 18" colored paper or fabric
balloon sticks, kite struts, or 1/8"
doweling

To make a pennant, cut a triangular shape from the paper or fabric. (Fabric will make a less stiff pennant.) Using available materials, decorate the pennant with the name and symbols of a saint. Then roll the 12" edge around a dowel, stick, or strut and fasten with glue, tape, or staples.

These pennants can be made smaller by starting with 6" x 9" or 9" x 12" paper, or they can be made much larger. For a very

small banner, use paper for the flag and attach it to a plastic drinking straw.

Two-Pole Banner

Materials (additional)

18" x 36" pieces of paper, fabric, or felt
2 36" poles

Begin by helping the participants decorate the 18" x 36" banner. Decorations can be drawn on the banner, or cut from construction paper or fabric and glued on.

To mount the banner, wrap one side of it around one pole and secure with staples, tape, or glue. Repeat with the other side. Tassels or ribbons could also be attached to the two poles.

Small Group Activity: Kitchen Band

Materials

    trash can lid and a wooden spoon
    metal pan lids and rubber spatulas
    bundt pan and a rubber spatula
    pair of 1' dowels or lengths of broom-
        stick
    cans or boxes, filled with rice or beans
        and sealed
    washboard and thimbles (for strumming
        the washboard)

Allow time for participants to experiment freely with these instruments. Then have the participants practice making rhythmic sounds together, at your signal. End the practice when most of the participants can make two beats of rhythmic sound at your signal.

Invite the participants to provide a rhythmic accompaniment to "When the saints go marching in." Signal the participants to make two beats of sound at each pause in the song. These pauses are marked by two asterisks (**). This song would make good music for a procession of pennants, banners and shields from the activities above.

1. Oh, when the saints**
   Go marching in**
   Oh, when the saints go marching in**
   Oh, Lord, I want to be in that number
   When the saints go marching in.**

2. Oh, when they gather**
   Round the throne**
   Oh, when they gather round the
       throne**
   Oh Lord, I want to be in that number
   When they gather round the throne.**

Leader's Resources: Multicultural Issues

● Additional saints representing different cultural and ethnic backgrounds can be celebrated in center or banner. Consider Blessed Kateri Tekakwitha (Native American), Blessed Juan Diego (Mexican), Saint Paul Miki (Japanese) or Saint Maximilian Kolbe (Polish).

● Foods representing different nationalities or ethnic origins of these and saints discussed in the Saints' Learning Centers could be brought to a pot luck meal following the liturgy for All Saints' Day.

Growing Together

Key Idea

All Christians, by virtue of their baptism, are members of the communion of saints.

Small Group Activity: Saints' Tags

Materials

    construction paper
    scissors
    glue
    felt pens
    masking tape

Divide the group of participants into pairs. Ask each participant to make a Saint Tag for his or her partner. Each tag should read: Saint *(name of partner)*.

Ask participants to decorate these tags with designs, pictures, or symbols that show the gifts and special qualities of this particular saint. If the group is not well-acquainted, allow a few minutes for partners to interview each other. Encourage older participants to help younger ones think of pictures, if necessary. Ask the participants to use masking tape to fasten the tags to clothing.

Small Group Activity: All Saints' Crowns

Materials

    6" x 18" strips of stiff, metallic gift wrap
       paper
    scissors
    clear tape
    stapler

Note: This activity is especially appropriate for children.

Each "saint" can make a crown to wear during the session. The crown is made of a row of human figures, like paper dolls, emphasizing the bond we have with each other as God's children.

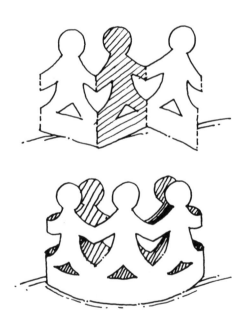

Fold a 6" x 18" strip of metallic gift wrap paper into six segments, each 6" x 3". Make the folds accordion-style, as you would in order to cut out a row of connected paper dolls. On the top segment, trace around the pattern on the following page.

Cut only along the solid lines, cutting through all the thicknesses at once. Unfold the paper and staple the two ends together to make a crown that fits snugly. Inside the crown, cover staples with two overlapping pieces of clear tape, to make the crown more comfortable.

Leader's Tip

You may prefer to produce a videotape rather than a slide show.

Large Group Activity: Slide Show

Materials

slides of parish members
taped reading of Psalm 145:1-18 and
    149:1-5
projector

Before the session prepare a slide presentation of the saints of the parish family at work. Photograph members of the parish community as they work, play, learn and worship together. Include pictures taken from parish members' daily lives.

At the parish family session, show the slide presentation. Play the tape of the psalms as an accompaniment. (When you

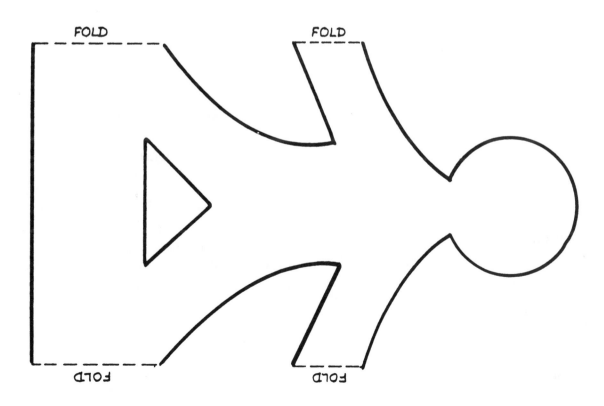

tape the reading, you might ask children to read some of the verses.)

Small Group Activity: Poster

Materials

> poster board
> felt
> pens
> crayons
> construction paper
> scissors
> glue

Use a felt pen to write "Welcome to the saints of *(name of the parish)*" across the top of the sheet of poster board.

Put the poster on a large table, together with the other materials listed. Invite passing participants to sign their names and baptismal dates on the poster, and to add designs to decorate it.

Encourage older participants to help younger participants write their names and dates. At the end of the session, hang the finished poster in a public part of the parish building.

Small Group Activity: Honoring Our Sainthood (for older participants)

Materials

> index cards
> pens or pencils
> basket

This activity, which is best for a small, well-acquainted group of participants, can be repeated several times. To begin, have each participant write his or her name on an index card. Collect the cards in a basket.

Ask each participant to draw a card and write on it the special qualities and gifts of the person named. After several minutes, have the participants return the cards to the individuals named on them.

Key Idea

All Christians are called to live holy lives that manifest the life of Jesus and follow the teachings of Jesus' Church.

The Beatitudes

Note: You may find this guide to the beatitudes helpful as you prepare activities for the session. As appropriate, share this information with participants.

The Greek words make it clear that these statements are to be heard as a congratulation for what already is—for the state into which the believer already has entered. The Greek word for blessed implies a godlike joy, a joy within one's self.

Blessed are the poor in spirit...
- those who feel a deep sense of spiritual poverty (see Is. 66:2)
- those who have detached themselves from possessions to follow Jesus
- those who put their entire trust in God and obey God completely

Blessed are those who mourn...
- those who have compassionate hearts, whose hearts are "broken" because of the world's suffering and one's own sin
- those who have endured deep sorrow

Blessed are the meek...
"Gentle" is the closest English translation for the original.
- those who are angry at moral injustice, but never angry for selfish reasons
- those who have the humility to see their own weakness and ignorance
- those who are totally God-controlled

Blessed are those who hunger and thirst for righteousness...
See Isaiah 55:1-2; John 4:14; John 6:51.
- those who fast and pray for the coming of the kingdom
- those who long for total goodness in the way a starving person longs for food

Blessed are the merciful...
- those who forgive others
- those who "get inside" others to feel their pain and to see with their eyes (as God did by becoming human)

Blessed are the pure in heart...
"Heart" in Hebrew means the seat of thought and will. This includes chastity, but is not limited to that.

- those who have pure motives, are sincere

Blessed are the peacemakers...
- those who work actively to *make peace*, not by evading issues but by conquering them
- those who establish right relationships among others

Blessed are those who are persecuted for righteousness' sake...
- those who are willing to be obedient to God and to serve as the conscience of the world, even at the cost of real consequences to themselves
- those who have given their lives to Christ

Persecution was an ever-present fact of life in the early Church.

Small Group Activity: Skits

Materials
Bible

Read Matthew 5:3-10 to the participants. Divide the group into eight small groups. Assign one of the Beatitudes to each group.

Ask each group to devise a skit showing a present day situation illustrating the assigned beatitude. Encourage each group to plan a role for every group member. Allow 10 minutes for preparation. Then ask each group to present its skit to the reassembled group.

Growing Together

▶ Small Group Activity: Wall Hanging (for older participants)

Materials

> 18" x 24" white drawing paper
> pencils
> felt pens

Ask one participant to use a pencil to draw, very lightly, a line that makes a free-form shape. The shape may be entirely abstract, or it may resemble an appropriate symbol, such as a crown.

Ask other participants to repeat the shape with a line drawn around the first shape, three inches away from it. Make as many of these larger, concentric shapes as necessary to bring the design within three inches of the edges of the paper.

Ask other participants to use different colors of felt pens to letter each of the Beatitudes on a penciled line. The penciled lines may be erased at the completion of the project.

▶ Small Group Activity: Discussion

Materials

> Bibles

Ask a participant to read Matthew 5:1-12. Discuss:

● Imagine yourself present when Jesus gave his Sermon on the Mount. Think what the conditions—economic, political, social and religious—of your life might have been. How would you have felt about this set of statements called the Beatitudes? Given the conditions of your real life today, how do you feel about the Beatitudes?

● Give examples of the ways Jesus manifested each of the Beatitudes in his life.

● What kind of person do you think is described by the Beatitudes? Do you know of anyone, past or present, who exemplifies one or more of the Beatitudes?

Leader's Resources: Outreach

● The Beatitudes could be used as a focus in presenting ideas for social outreach. Participants might want to list specific ways in which they could put into action the call of the Beatitudes: turn away from consumerism toward a simpler life, seek peaceful resolution of conflict, comfort those who mourn, etc.

● Consider exploring the commitment to peace and justice of contemporary Catholic holy men and women in the Saints' Learning Centers: Dorothy Day, Thomas Merton, Mother Teresa, Oscar Romero or the martyrs of El Salvador.

● Encourage support and participation in social action programs beyond the parish by distributing publications from the diocesan Peace and Justice Office or from Catholic Charities, Catholic Workers, Catholic Relief Services, etc.

Closing Prayer

If the group includes young children, close with the Our Father or prayers or blessings chosen from the Feast of All Saints in the Roman Catholic Sacramentary. (See the Proper of Saints, page 728, or #15 from the Votive Masses, page 949.)

If the group is older, use the Scripture Meditation below before the Our Father or other selected prayer.

▶ Scripture Meditation

(Ask everyone to find a comfortable position for 15 minutes of prayer. Ask participants to close their eyes and visualize the gospel scene as you slowly read to them the meditation below.)

On a mountain side, away from the crowds, Jesus is seated with his disciples. He looks at them with great love—those who have followed faithfully. It is evident in the way he gathers them to him that he takes pleasure in their presence.

Once more he begins to teach them:

"Happy are those who know they are spiritually poor; the Kingdom of heaven belongs to them!"

He stops to answer questions. When it seems that his listeners understand, he goes on,

"Happy are those who mourn; God will comfort them! Happy are those who are humble; they will receive what God has promised!"

Again he stops to answer questions. He has more to say,

"Happy are the merciful...the pure in heart...Happy are those who work for peace; they will be called God's children!"

Gently, gently, he leads them into the ways of the kingdom. His style is not that of the lawgiver, or judge. He teaches the ways of the kingdom by invitation... inviting his listeners to follow a pathway whose end is blessing and happiness.

The disciples listen closely. Their faithfulness witnesses to their love for Jesus and their willingness to follow him. And Jesus responds to this small band of loyal followers...taking pleasure in them...letting his love flow out to them.

They do not know what lies ahead. All they know is that they are with the Lord ...loving him...listening to him...following him. He will give them all the help they need to do what he asks of them.

(At the end of the reading, pause, and then ask, "Is this all that is necessary to us today?" Allow five minutes for silent reflection on this question. Then ask participants to share their reflections with the group. Close by praying together the Our Father or other selected prayer.)

Thanksgiving

Introduction and Information

Both the United States and Canada celebrate the agricultural harvest and other blessings of our life with an annual feast day in the fall. These feast days are not only festive celebrations, but a time to recall our responsibilities as stewards as well.

Although regional variations of dates and observances arose in later years, George Washington declared the first national day of Thanksgiving in 1789. In 1939 Congress fixed the date of Thanksgiving in the United States as the fourth Thursday in November. Canada celebrated its first national Thanksgiving in 1879, and now observes the day on the second Monday of each October.

Thanksgiving was the first holiday celebrated by the Puritan settlers of Massachusetts. The three-day celebration, held after the harvest of 1621, combined two aspects of similar celebrations from England and Europe: a harvest festival and a public thanksgiving for a specific occasion of deliverance.

A Harvest Festival

Harvest festivals, of course, are found in agricultural communities across the globe and throughout history. Three Jewish festivals—Passover, Pentecost and Tabernacles—had connections to agricultural events. The first occurred at the time of new births in the animal flocks; the second at the harvest of grain and the third at the time of new wine.

Many different harvest festivals were celebrated by the medieval Church. One such day was Lammas Day in England, which commemorated the harvest of grain with church services and feasting. Though the Puritans did not retain Lammas Day, their own harvest celebration did retain such festival traditions as prayer, feasting and games. Even our contemporary celebration of Thanksgiving includes these traditions, though now the games are often watched rather than played!

A Festival of Gratitude

The second aspect of Thanksgiving, gratitude for a specific event, is also widespread in human societies. Indeed, such thanksgivings gave rise to the characteristic liturgies of both Judaism and Christianity, as in the Passover Seder and the Christian Eucharist.

Throughout the middle ages, days of special thanksgiving were held to praise God for deliverance from famine, plague or war. This tradition *was* preserved by Puritan settlers and put to its first use in the autumn of 1621. In the United States today, we celebrate Thanksgiving as a national holiday, but our Catholic heritage makes us aware of our special call to lives of gratitude that culminate in our celebration of the Eucharist and in lives of stewardship.

A Festival of Stewardship

Our daily commitments to stewardship should permeate our celebration of Thanksgiving. We give thanks to God for blessings of food and freedom, but we realize that such blessings demand our responsible use of every gift, every resource. Our gratitude should inspire us with renewed determination to work for justice and peace for all.

Thanksgiving Day invites us to actions of remembrance, gratitude and stewardship. Let these be the hallmarks of our celebration, and the hallmarks of our lives in Christ as we pray, "Thank you, Lord."

Help! How do I plan this session?

How will I publicize this session?

_____

_____

How many people do I think might participate? _____

What are the ages of the participants?

_____

Where will we hold the session?

_____

Which recommended activities would work best with this particular group of participants? (Remember, we provide more activities than most groups can use in a single session. Pick the few that will work for your group.)

_____

_____

_____

_____

_____

_____

_____

Volunteers

to do	names	phone numbers
planning:		
preparation and set-up:		
activity leaders:		
clean-up:		

Growing Together

Session Plan

Gathering Prayer

An appropriate song for this session could be "Eat This Bread" by Jacques Berthier.

Key Idea

Thanksgiving is a national holiday, appropriately enriched with certain traditional foods, games and entertainments.

Small Group Activity: Corn Cooking

Materials

assorted varieties of cornmeal: yellow, white, coarse, etc.

mixing bowls

wooden spoons

cookie sheet, preferably non-stick

maple syrup or honey

measuring cups

3-quart saucepan

soup or cereal bowls

spoons

ears of corn, preferably with husks attached

Optional:
aluminum foil

Native Americans knew how to grow, harvest and cook this important food. Invite participants to make corn dishes that the original inhabitants of the land, or immigrant settlers, might have made from the harvest.

Corn Pone

Put cornmeal in a mixing bowl. Do not fill the bowl more than one-third full. Ask participants to slowly stir in water until the cornmeal has a consistency similar to soft modeling dough.

Participants turn the dough onto a cookie sheet, then pat the dough until it is evenly spread onto the sheet. Bake a 1/4-inch thick corn pone at 350° for about 20 minutes, or until the pone is cooked through. Serve by breaking into pieces. Offer maple syrup or honey for sweetening.

Corn Mush

Mix two cups cornmeal with two cups cold water. Bring four additional cups of water to boil in the saucepan. Stir in the cornmeal and cold water. Participants take turns stirring the cornmeal over very low heat for 20-30 minutes, or until the cornmeal has cooked into a thin porridge. Serve in bowls with maple syrup or honey.

Roasted Corn

Participants carefully peel the husks from each ear of corn, leaving all the husks attached. Participants remove all the corn silk, then wrap ears back in their husks. Roast the corn in a 350° oven for about 20-30 minutes. If no ears of corn with husks are available, participants can wrap the corn in aluminum foil before baking.

Small Group Activity: Thanksgiving Twenty Questions (game)

Invite participants to play a variation of this traditional game; the original game was known to Puritan children. In the traditional game, one participant thinks of an object, and tells the other participants whether the object is an animal, a vegetable or a mineral. The Thanksgiving variation is to ask that the objects be something for which the participant is grateful.

The other participants take turns asking up to 20 questions in order to guess the name of the objects. Each question must be answered only with "yes" or "no." Possible questions:
- Is it a person?
- Is it bigger than you?
- Can you eat it?
- Is there one in this room?
- Can you buy it?

Small Group Activity: Thanksgiving Skits

Ask participants to work in groups of four to eight people to invent skits for Thanksgiving day. Ask that each group build its skit around an event for which they are grateful. Situations could include:
- a child finds something that had been lost
- a person or group of people escapes from danger
- someone makes a new friend
- one of the assigned gospel readings for Thanksgiving day, Luke 17:11-20 (the story of the ten lepers)

Invite groups to present their finished skits to the other participants.

Small Group Activity: Story Pairs

Invite participants to form pairs, then ask each pair to work together to write a Thanksgiving story. Encourage older participants to pair with younger participants.

Ask that all participants accept one another's contributions as spoken, including digressions or grammatical errors. For example, one pair might write:

> A child loses a mitten. It was her brand new mitten. I just got a new mitten, too. She lost it in the street. She couldn't find it nowhere.

After 15-20 minutes, reconvene the larger group. Invite pairs to read their stories aloud to the group.

Growing Together

Leader's Resources: Multicultural Issues

- Participants could learn to say "thank you" in various languages represented by the group. They could then practice these new words throughout the session, whenever appreciation was called for.
- In addition to these corn foods, invite participants to bring a bread to share that represents their ethnic or cultural tradition. These breads would also reinforce the connection of Thanksgiving to the Eucharist.
- When sharing bread, participants could sing "Pan de Vida" by Bob Hurd.

Key Idea

Thanksgiving celebrates the agricultural harvest.

Small Group Activity: Pumpkin Rolling (outdoor game)

Materials

pumpkins, about 15 lbs. each, 1 per team

chairs, 1 per team

If you have a stretch of grass, and a stretch of fine weather, hold a Pumpkin Roll outdoors. Decide on a starting line, perhaps a sidewalk edging the grass. Place the chairs in a line 25-50 feet away. Allow at least 10 feet of space between chairs.

Divide the participants into teams of eight players. Give each team a pumpkin. At your signal, the first player on each team rolls the team's pumpkin on the grass to the team's chair, around the team's chair, and back to the starting line. Players may use only their heads to roll the pumpkins.

When the pumpkin reaches the starting line, the next player takes the pumpkin and rolls it to the chair. Continue until all the players on one team have rolled the pumpkin.

Preschoolers and kindergartners will have more fun if you eliminate the competitive element. Allow them simply to roll the pumpkins on the grass, perhaps playing a rolling version of "catch" with older partners.

Small Group Activity: Squash Soup

Materials

2 acorn squash
sharp knife
food mill, food processor or blender
6-quart saucepan
wooden spoons
milk, up to 1/2 gallon
salt and pepper
nutmeg
soup bowls
spoons

Before the session use the knife to pierce the shell of each squash in two or three places. Bake in a 350° oven for one hour, or until the squash is soft. Cut open and let cool.

Participants can remove the seeds and puree the squash in a food mill, food processor or blender. Ask the participants to stir in milk until the squash puree has the consistency of soup.

To serve, heat the soup over medium heat, stirring frequently, until hot. Season to taste with salt, pepper and nutmeg.

Note: These amounts and methods are suitable for a group of six to eight participants.

Small Group Activity: Table Decorations

Invite participants to make table decorations to take home, to decorate the parish building, to give to shut-ins of the parish family or to use at community Thanksgiving meals.

Apple Candle Holders (for older participants)

Materials

paring knives
apples
dinner candles

Participants use knives to partially hollow out each apple core. Ask each participant to work carefully to make a recess just large enough to securely hold a dinner candle.

Harvest Baskets

Materials

shopping bags, preferably with handles
scissors
nuts
multicolored corn
colorful gourds
red apples
small breadbaskets (preferably oval, 2"-3" high, 10"-12" long)
Optional:
floral foam

Invite participants to collect decorative plan materials on a short walk outdoors. Look for fallen leaves, seedpods and dried grasses or weeds. Make sure you gather only from streets or empty lots, not from parks or yards.

Growing Together

Back at the parish, have ready additional decorative materials, nuts, corn, gourds and apples. Invite participants to work in groups of four to six members to make colorful arrangements of these autumn and harvest materials.

Give each group a basket in which to make its arrangement. If desired, participants can tape floral foam inside the basket to better secure inserted grasses, leaves and weeds.

Large Group Activity: Interviews

Consider inviting speakers representing the agricultural community to prepare 5-10 minute talks for the parish family. Ask speaks to describe their work in growing and gathering food. Possible guests might include local small farmers or harvesters, such as members of the United Farm Workers.

One way to locate small farmers is by contacting produce managers of local grocery stores or food cooperatives. These sources, and the farmers themselves, may be able to provide you with contacts to the community of agricultural workers.

Encourage participants to ask questions of these speakers, and be sure to invite the speakers to join in any festivities or refreshments you have prepared.

Key Idea

Thanksgiving is a good day to celebrate all the blessings of our life, especially the sacrament through which we particularly offer thanks: the Eucharist.

Small Group Activity: Thanks Lists (for older participants)

Materials

paper
pens or pencils

Ask each participant to make a list of things for which he or she is thankful. Allow 5-10 minutes.

Then ask participants to mark their lists by following these instructions.
- Circle the three items for which you are most thankful.
- Evaluate whether each item on your list is a necessity of life, or an extra blessing in your life. Mark necessities with the letter *N* and extras with the letter *X*.
- Evaluate whether the joy of each item on your list comes from people or from things. Mark items centered on people with the letter *P* and items centered on things with the letter *T*.
- Evaluate whether each item on your list occurs frequently or rarely in your life. Mark frequently occurring items with

the letter *F* and rarely occurring items with the letter *R*.

Divide participants into small groups of four or five members each to discuss these questions:

- What discoveries did we make about what causes us to feel thankful?
- How could we increase these feelings in our own lives? In the lives of our families? In the life of our parish family?
- What do you think this list might have included if it had been made by Jesus?

Small Group Activity: Thanks Basket (game)

Materials

basket
3" x 5" cards, preferably unruled
felt pens

Seat participants in a circle with the basket in the middle. Ask each participant to take cards and a felt pen. (You can limit the length of the game by specifying that each participant take a certain number of cards, such as two.)

The first participant draws a quick sketch of something for which he or she is thankful, and places it in the basket, saying, "I thank God for *(name the choice)*."

The second participant repeats the actions, saying, "I thank God for *(name of the first participant's choice, followed by the choice of the second participant. The second participant sketches his or her own choice only.)*"

Play continues around the circle. The pictures help younger participants remember the names of the items. Encourage all participants to work together to keep the game going; participants can help each other draw the pictures and name the items.

End the play at an arbitrarily chosen point, such as when each player has had two turns.

Small Group Activity: Oral Biographies

Materials

copies of the Interview Question Sheet, found on the next page
2 chairs
Optional:
tape recorders
blank tapes

Before the session arrange for six of the older members of the parish and community to be interviewed. Ask six participants between ages eleven and fifteen to serve as interviewers. Give each interviewer a copy of the Interview Question Sheet (on next page).

At the session, set up two chairs for each pair of an interviewer and a person being interviewed. Invite other participants to be audiences at each center. When the prepared interview is over, the interviewer invites additional questions from the audience.

Growing Together

If you have recording equipment available, either audio or video, you can tape these sessions. Save the tapes as oral history resources for the parish and community. After your own questions are done, invite questions from the audience.

Questions:

What is your name?

What was your day like when you were my age?

How did you first come to our community?

How has the community changed since then?

When and how were you baptized?

How has the Church changed since then?

How did you celebrate Thanksgiving when you were my age?

For what did you feel thankful then? For what do you feel thankful today?

Do you have another question for your partner? Write that question here:

Small Group Activity: Reflections and Meditations

Materials

> drawing paper
> pencils, pens and felt pens

Invite participants to share memories of the first Thanksgiving they remember. Then ask participants to share memories of the last Thanksgiving they remember. Discuss:

- How are our first stories different from our last stories?
- What different stories could we have next year? In twenty years?
- What stories could we hear if we asked our pets to tell what Thanksgiving is like?
- What stories could we hear if we asked someone sad to tell us what Thanksgiving is like?
- What stories could we hear if we asked someone without a home to tell us what Thanksgiving is like?

Invite participants to work alone, in pairs or in groups of three to imagine Thanksgiving stories from other voices. Ask participants to write or draw their stories on drawing paper.

After 10-15 minutes work, invite participants to share their stories. Discuss:

- How could the stories we have heard and imagined change our own Thanksgiving celebrations?

Invite participants to close with prayer for themselves and those people they have discovered in their stories.

Small Group Activity: Murals

Materials

> Bible
> roll of butcher paper
> scissors
> tape
> felt pens
> crayons

Read aloud Deuteronomy 8:1-3, 6-10. Invite participants to make murals, one showing the Israelites' good life, and one showing our own good life. Ask each participant to work on one mural.

Tape two strips of butcher paper onto the floor, or onto long tables. Provide felt pens and crayons for drawing.

Ask participants working on the first mural to draw everything they think the Israelites might have found—fruit, land, animals, etc.—in God's promised land. Ask the participants working on the second mural to draw everything they find good—food, toys, places, etc.—in their own land. Ask both groups to include drawings of God's people in both murals.

When each group is finished discuss:
- What do you like in each mural?
- What do God's people do in each mural?
- How can God's people give thanks for the good things in these murals?
- How can we act on our ideas for ways to give thanks today?

Growing Together

The murals can be used to decorate the worship space at the parish Thanksgiving Day Mass.

Small Group Activity: Bread Making

Materials

ingredients for any simple bread recipe (look in a favorite cookbook) or defrosted frozen ready-made bread dough

Participants talk about the blessings of the Eucharist as they make simple bread. The finished bread can be baked in a parish oven or a toaster oven, or taken home for final baking.

Ask participants to consider the special part bread plays in the Mass. Discuss:

- What special foods do our different families eat at Thanksgiving?
- What good things does the Thanksgiving meal give our families?
- What special food do we receive during the Mass?
- What good things does the Mass give our parish family?

Invite participants to celebrate the gift of bread by making some.

Either follow with the participants a simple bread recipe you bring, or distribute small amounts of ready-made dough to each participant. Invite participants to shape these handfuls into bagels, pretzels, alpha-

bet letters, crosses, bread sticks—anything goes!

Bake the bread for immediate sharing, or set it aside to rise until participants leave for home.

Key Idea

We are called to be stewards of God's blessings.

Large Group Activity: Food Collection

Materials

shopping bags or baskets
large table

Several weeks **before the session** check with the parish food pantry or with a local agency that ministers to the hungry to find out what food items are most needed. Run notices in parish bulletins, asking participants to bring needed foods to this Thanksgiving session.

At the session ask participants to sort and collect the food for easy distribution through the pantry. Help participants make arrangements for delivering the food.

For a litany of thanks, ask participants to form a circle around the table of food items. Ask each participant to choose an item and pray:

> For *(name the item)* for the hungry, we thank you, Lord.

The other participants respond:

> Thank you, Lord.

Conclude by praying:

> God, we thank you for feeding your people manna in the wilderness. We thank you for feeding the 5,000 with two fish and five loaves of bread. We thank you for feeding us in our daily lives and at your table, with the Bread of Life. Help us to share our abundance with all your people who are hungry. *Amen.*

Small Group Activity: Thank Offerings

Materials

> coins in a box (pennies, nickels, dimes or quarters)
> soft drink cans or empty frozen juice containers
> Contact paper
> felt pens

Before the session cover one can or container with Contact paper. Decorate the covered container with felt pens.

At the session place the coins in a box in front of you. Let the coins run through your fingers to catch the attention of the participants. Explain that we can use coins to say *thank you* to God, if we give these

Growing Together

coins for those in need, through Catholic Charities, Food for the Poor, Catholic Relief Services, etc. Then drop a coin into the decorated container.

Pass around the box of coins and the container. Ask each participant to say *thank you* to God, in words and with a coin in the container.

Then invite participants to make their own thank offering cans to take home. Ask participants to talk about ways they could use these cans to become more aware of God's blessings in their lives, and to share with those in need.

Small Group Activity: Bible Study (for older participants)

Materials

Bibles

Ask a participant to read Matthew 6:25-33. Discuss:
● This passage is part of Jesus' Sermon on the Mount. What message can we, as disciples of Jesus today, draw from this passage?
— Does our understanding differ from the disciples' understanding of Jesus' message? Why or why not?
— What attitudes do you think Jesus addressed in this passage?
— Jesus used the examples of food and clothing to illustrate his message. What other examples could be added to these?

● Read Matthew 25:21. How do you reconcile Jesus' command not to worry over tomorrow (Mt. 6:34) with Jesus' command to be faithful stewards (Mt. 25:21)?
— What blessings has God bestowed on us in Jesus Christ?
— How can we be faithful stewards of those blessings?

Divide the participants into small groups of four or five to discuss these questions:
● How would a parish budget show that concern for the kingdom of God was the parish's first priority?
● How would a family budget show that concern for the kingdom of God was the family's first priority?

Leader's Resources: Outreach

The celebration of Thanksgiving Day is never complete without sharing our abundance with others. Invite those organizations that minister to those in need to speak to the group about their work and about the need to continue assistance beyond the holiday season.

Serving food, in person, to the hungry is one highly effective way to develop a sense of stewardship and service. Encourage participants to serve in a parish or community soup kitchen. If there is a Thanksgiving meal for those in need, try to take part with other members of the parish family. If no such meal exists in the community, is the parish being called to begin one?

Closing Prayer

- You can choose a closing prayer from the Thanks Basket or Food Collection activities in this session.
- The "Blessing of Produce" on pages 170-171 from *Catholic Household Blessings and Prayers* can be adapted from its intended use on August 15 to a Thanksgiving blessing during this session. The prayer of thanksgiving after meals (pp. 56-59) could also be used.

- The traditional Catholic blessing before meals ("Bless us, O Lord, and these thy gifts which we are about to receive from your bounty, through Christ our Lord. *Amen.*") could be recited by the group before enjoying the food prepared for this session.

Invite participants to work together to create a Litany of Thanksgiving. Ask participants to work in pairs writing one way to complete this prayer sentence:

Lord, we thank you for...

When participants are done writing, pray the litany by having each pair of participants in turn read aloud their prayer. The entire group can respond to each litany prayer by praying:

Thank you, Lord.

Advent

Introduction and Information

Advent, the first season of the Church year, begins on the fourth Sunday before Christmas. (This is the Sunday falling on or nearest November 30.) Varying from 22 to 28 days, the season ends on Christmas Eve. The liturgical colors for Advent are purple and blue.

We spend this time preparing for the celebration of Christmas. We make gifts and buy them. We cover the presents, in wrappings plain and fancy, making each gift as secret as the child who grew in Mary's womb.

We prepare and receive cards, wishing each friend and loved one a happy and holy celebration of Christmas. Our houses are perhaps more fragrant now than at any other time of year, with a heady mix of the aromas of candle wax, evergreens and spices.

Even our toddlers, even the unchurched, are certain that the coming Christmas is a time of great joy. We may not like canned carols at the malls and plastic Santas on the lawns, but we do need to understand the longing for joy that prompts them. We need to find ways to enrich our own and our community's preparations with the deeper meanings of Advent.

Advent Means *Coming*

We need to remember, for example, that the word ***advent*** means coming. During Advent, we prepare for the celebration of the coming of Jesus as a babe in Bethlehem.

That birth fulfilled both the words of Israel's prophets and the events in Israel's history that speak of God's saving grace. Thus, the Church has appointed scriptures for Advent that tell of God's promises to the people of Israel, especially prophecies that suggest the coming of a Messiah and a messianic age.

You are God's, Abraham heard in an alien land, ***and God will be yours***, promised Isaiah. Every covenant and prophecy—from the exodus to the foretelling of the nations' return to Jerusalem—recalled the promise of union with God. In Jesus, the promise is fulfilled.

During Advent, we recall and honor those who prepared the way for Jesus, and especially those who welcomed his birth, Zechariah, Elizabeth, Mary, Joseph and others. We hear the stories of preparation. We sing carols of expectation.

Growing Together

But our expectation is not limited to the past events of Bethlehem. Jesus is coming, not only once to Bethlehem, but today in word and sacrament. Jesus is coming, not only 2000 years ago, but again, in great glory, at the end of all time. Thus, in Advent, we also read scriptures that tell of an ultimate judgment, the end of this age and a new reign of the kingdom of God.

These scriptures suggest questions: Might Jesus' second coming encompass both an outward, physical event and an inner event of the mind and heart? Indeed, it is often the apocalyptic events of our lives that bring us from a time of "running our own shows" (at great distance from God) into a new, deeper relationship with God.

A Season of Paradox

Clearly, Advent is a season of paradox. We have inherited this two-fold emphasis on joyful expectation and somber repentance from the early Church.

In the fourth century, Christians began celebrating Christmas as a religious festival, replacing the older pagan feast of the Unconquered Sun. It follows that in part of Christendom, the Church sought to make Advent a period of joy, glowing with the power of the Son of God.

In other places, the Church directed candidates who would be received into the Church on Epiphany, January 6, to fast during the preceding midwinter weeks. For this reason, Advent eventually became a time of penitent preparation for all Christians.

So now we watch and wait. We watch and wait as the days of Advent run to Christmas. We watch and wait as the Church prepares place and song and heart for our infant Savior.

We watch and wait for he who comes to us, in scripture and in Eucharist, who feeds us with his life. We watch and wait for the one who comes to fill all things, to make the whole creation new.

We watch and wait for Jesus, and he is coming.

Help! How do I plan this session?

How will I publicize this session?

_____

_____

How many people do I think might participate? _____

What are the ages of the participants?

_____

Where will we hold the session?

_____

Which recommended activities would work best with this particular group of participants? (Remember, we provide more activities than most groups can use in a single session. Pick a few that will work for your group.)

_____

_____

_____

_____

_____

_____

_____

Volunteers

to do	names	phone numbers
planning:		
preparation and set-up:		
activity leaders:		
clean-up:		

Growing Together

Session Plan

Gathering Prayer

Begin the celebration by singing together "O Come, O Come, Emmanuel." Other choices might include "Patience, People" (John Foley, SJ), "Make Straight the Way (Tom Conry) or "Magnificat" (Christopher Walker).

Key Idea

The word *advent* means coming. During Advent, we prepare both for the coming of Jesus as a babe in Bethlehem and his coming in great glory at the end of all time. Advent also keeps before us the coming of Jesus here and now in word and sacrament.

Small Group Activity: Paper Banners

Materials

Bibles
6' sheets of white butcher paper, 1 per group
scissors
large sheets of tissue paper in various colors
rubber cement
empty margarine tubs (to hold rubber cement)
small house-painting brushes
black felt markers

Begin by asking everyone which Church season comes just before Christmas. Explain that the word Advent means coming and that this activity will help everyone learn who is coming and when. Plan to count off in order to divide into random groups of six to 10 people each, making sure that each group includes both children and adults.

Before the session write out one of the questions below for each group, making duplicates if necessary. In the session, divide into groups and furnish each group with materials and one of the questions.

Directions to the groups: Read your question aloud in your group. Look up answers in your Bibles, adults helping children as needed. Answer your question and decide how the group will quickly make a paper banner to illustrate your answer. (Tearing the tissue paper into large shapes will work more easily than cutting out many small shapes.) On your banner write the word Advent and write phrases from scripture that answer your question.

Leader's Tip

 As you give instructions for an activity, jot key words on newsprint or chalkboard for the participants to refer to as they work.

 Key words for this activity might be: read and answer question, illustrate answer, write Advent and phrases from scripture on banner.

Questions:

Group 1: When and how did Jesus come to us in the very first Advent? (Matthew 1:18-25; Luke 1:26-38; John 1:1-5, 14)

Group 2: When and how will Jesus come to us in the future at what we call his second coming? (Matthew 25:1-13; Mark 13:24-27; Luke 21:25-28; 1 Corinthians 15:20-28)

Group 3: How does Jesus come to us here and now in the Eucharist? (Matthew 26:26-29; Mark 14:22-25; Luke 22:14-20; John 6:32-40; 1 Corinthians 11:23-26)

After everyone has finished, reassemble and ask someone from each group to read the group's question and explain how its banner answers the questions.

Large Group Activity: Giving Tree

Materials

white, unlined 3" x 5" cards
a Christmas tree
red ribbon or yarn
hole punch
felt pens
or
a 3' x 6' paper silhouette of a Christmas tree
gummed note pad
felt pens

Before the session contact the leaders of your parish's outreach ministries. Ask each leader to prepare a list of items needed for the poor, including inexpensive items, such as soap and toilet paper. (You may want to expand this activity to include lists of items from community service agencies.)

Ask a group of people to help you write each item desired on a 3" x 5" card, then punch a hole in the corner of each card. Attach the cards to your parish's Christmas tree by red ribbon or yarn that you string through the holes. Or, if you are using a paper silhouette of a tree, write each item on a slip of gummed paper and stick the notes to the tree.

At your parish family session, invite each participant to meet Jesus, who comes to us in the needy, by choosing a slip of paper and bringing the needed item to church during Advent.

Growing Together

Leader's Resources: Outreach

- The Advent season lends itself particularly well to giving to others. Beyond the Giving Tree activity, invite participants to take advantage of the many opportunities offered by most parishes to assist those in need through food collections, financial donations, wrapping and distributing gifts, etc. Invite persons from parish or diocesan social service organizations to speak to the group, emphasizing the ongoing needs of the poor.
- Families could design their own decorative "collection basket" to use at home for daily or weekly financial contributions to the poor.
- Consider using litany-style prayers of petition for the poor and needy during today's closing prayer. Use the liturgical formula, "We pray to the Lord." "Lord, hear our prayer." A sung version ("O God, Hear Us" or the Spanish "Te Rogamus, Señor," both by Bob Hurd, OCP, Portland, OR) would be particularly effective.

▶ Small Group Activity: Creating a Newspaper

Materials

Bibles
paper
pens or pencils
felt pens
crayons
18" x 24" newsprint paper
tape

Divide the participants into three groups. Ask each group to make one newspaper about the good news of Jesus' coming.

Ask the first group to make a newspaper about the coming of Jesus as a baby to Bethlehem. Refer the group to Luke 2:1-20.

Ask the second group to make a newspaper about the coming of Jesus to us today in word and sacrament. Suggest interviewing each other about experiences with Jesus in word and sacrament.

For example, the participants might ask each other:
- What makes you feel close to Jesus?
- What are your favorite stories of Jesus and why?
- What do you remember about your First Communion?
- What does the bread mean to you? What does the wine mean to you?

Ask the third group to make a newspaper about the coming of Jesus at the end of time. Suggest the use of the prophecies in Isaiah 25:6-9, Matthew 25:31-45 and Revelation 21:1-4 as resources.

Suggest to all the groups that their newspapers might contain:
editorials
cartoons
interviews
opinion polls
drawings

Encourage children to draw pictures to illustrate the newspapers. Ask each group to mount its finished items on a sheet of newsprint as though laying out a newspaper page. Tape the finished newspapers to a wall.

Leader's Tip

This activity could be adapted to produce videos instead of newspapers! You'll need knowledgeable help, appropriate equipment and lots of time.

Key Idea

The birth of Jesus fulfilled the prophetic acts of God in Israel's history and the words of her prophets.

Background Notes:
The Jesse Tree

Jesse was the father of King David and both were ancestors of Jesus. Many years after Jesse lived, the prophet Isaiah told of a new tree that would grow from the stump of Jesse. "The royal line of David is like a tree that has been cut down; but just as new branches sprout from a stump, so a new king will arise from among David's descendants" (Is. 11:1).

A Jesse Tree can be an evergreen tree, a fabric wall hanging in the shape of a tree or a bare branch anchored in a pot of rocks. The custom is to add a decoration to the tree each day during Advent. The decorations are symbols of Jesse and other men and women of the Old Testament who prepared the way for Jesus.

This chapter includes directions for making Jesse Tree decorations and a booklet to use along with the decorations. In your parish family session, invite participants to make the booklets and symbols to use at home. Or make decorations to use on a Jesse Tree for your parish.

Small Group Activity:
Jesse Tree Books

Materials

white 8-1/2" x 11" paper, 7 sheets per person

8-1/2" x 11" purple construction paper, 1 sheet per person

pink yarn or satin ribbon

hole punch

scissors

rubber cement or glue stick

list of symbols (see next page), 1 copy per person

felt pens or crayons or scraps of construction paper

Before the session make a copy of the list of symbols for each participant. At your session briefly explain the custom of the Jesse Tree and invite each person to make a Jesse Tree book to take home. Plan to demonstrate as you give directions.

Growing Together

Directions for making a book: Fold seven white sheets of paper in half. Tuck each sheet inside another. (The size of the book will be 8-1/2" long and 5-1/2" wide.)

Fold a sheet of construction paper in like fashion and put this around the pages as a cover. Punch two holes near the spine of the booklet. Run a piece of yarn through the holes and tie the booklet together.

Continue: Number the pages 1-28. Take the sheet that lists the Jesse Tree symbols and cut along the solid lines so that you have a slip of paper for each day of Advent. Glue a slip to each page, in consecutive order from 1 to 28. Glue each slip near the bottom of the page so that you have room to draw the appropriate symbol.

Draw each symbol or cut it out of construction paper and glue it on the appropriate page.

Jesse Tree Symbols for Booklets

Day 1: Jesse

symbol: the Jesse Tree
reading: Isaiah 11:1-10

Day 2: creation

symbol: the world
reading: Genesis 1:1-2:3

Day 3: Adam and Eve

symbol: Adam and Eve
reading: Genesis 3:1-24

Day 4: Noah

symbol: ark
reading: Genesis 8:13-9:17

Day 5: Abraham

symbol: stars
reading: Genesis 12:1-3, 15:1-6

Day 6: Sarah

symbol: bread
reading: Genesis 18:1-15, 21:1-7

Day 7: Isaac

symbol: ram
reading: Genesis 22:1-14

Day 8: Jacob

symbol: ladder
reading: Genesis 28:10-17

Day 9: Joseph

symbol: coat of many colors
reading: Genesis 45:4-15

Day 10: Moses

symbol: stone tablets
reading: Exodus 13:3-22

Day 11: Miriam

symbol: tambourine
reading: Exodus 15:1-21

Day 12: Aaron

symbol: hand of blessing
reading: Numbers 6:22-27, Leviticus 9:22-24

Day 13: Joshua

symbol: ram's horn
reading: Joshua 6:2-16, 20

Day 14: Rahab

symbol: scarlet cord
reading: Joshua 2:1-21

Day 15: Ruth

symbol: ear of grain
reading: Ruth 1:1-18

Day 16: Samuel

symbol: lamp
reading: 1 Samuel 3:1-19

Day 17: David

symbol: harp
reading: 1 Samuel 16:1-13

Day 18: Solomon

symbol: crown
reading: 2 Chronicles 5:1-14

Day 19: Elijah

symbol: jars of meal and oil
reading: 1 Kings 17:1-6

Day 20: Elisha

symbol: flaming wheel
reading: 2 Kings 2:1-15

Day 21: Isaiah

symbol: throne
reading: Isaiah 35:1-10

Day 22: Jeremiah

symbol: almond branch
reading: Jeremiah 1:11-12, 31:31-34

Day 23: Ezekiel

symbol: shepherd's crook
reading: Ezekiel 34:1-16

Day 24: Ezra and Nehemiah

symbol: scroll of Torah
reading: Nehemiah 8:1-12

Day 25: Mary

symbol: Mary and dove
reading: Luke 1:26-38

Day 26: Joseph

symbol: carpenters' tools
reading: Matthew 1:18-25

Day 27: Jesus

symbol: chi rho (the first letters of Christ in Greek) and manger
reading: Luke 2:1-21

Day 28: You

symbol: the finished Jesse Tree
reading: John 15:5-17

Jesse Tree Symbols

Jesse

Creation

Adam and Eve

Noah

Abraham

Sarah

Isaac

Jacob

Joseph

Jesse Tree Symbols (continued)

Moses

Miriam

Aaron

Joshua

Rahab

Ruth

Samuel

David

Solomon

Jesse Tree Symbols (continued)

Elijah

Elisha

Isaiah

Jeremiah

Ezekiel

Ezra and Nehemiah

Mary

Joseph

Jesus

Small Group Activity: Jesse Tree Ornaments

Materials

> felt, in assorted colors
> scissors
> glue
> *Optional:*
> sequins, glitter, pom-poms, etc.
> prepared slips of paper in basket

Invite participants to make a set of Jesse Tree ornaments to use at home on a bare branch tree, felt tree or evergreen. Provide the list of symbols as given above, but invite participants to invent their own, if they wish.

Or, if you prefer, ask each person to make an ornament to hang on a Jesse Tree for your parish. To assign the symbols, write each on a slip of paper, making duplicates as necessary, and pass the basket.

Suggest a collage technique for constructing the ornaments. For example: The crown for David could be cut from yellow felt, then decorated with glued-on scraps of felt in bright colors or with sequins or glitter.

Large Group Activity: Mural of the New Creation

Materials

> Bibles
> 10' long sheet of butcher paper
> crayons or felt markers or colored chalk
> chalkboard and chalk or newsprint and
>   marker
> masking tape

Read Isaiah 65:17-25 to the participants, inviting everyone to read along silently. Discuss:

● Why do we read about God's new creation in Advent?
● What will we find in the new creation?
● How would you feel living there?

(List answers on chalkboard or newsprint.)

Mention, if no one else has, that Jesus brings the new creation to God's people. Invite everyone to work together to make a mural that illustrates Jesus' bringing the new creation.

Ask for a volunteer to draw each item on your list of what we will find in the new creation. Invite participants to draw this scene using crayons, felt markers or colored chalk on a long sheet of butcher paper that you have taped to the wall. (Make sure that it is within reach of the children.)

Key Idea

In Advent, we remember those who prepared the way for Jesus, and those who first welcomed his birth. Let us gather not just to hear once again, but to experience, the story of the true Lord of Christmas.

Growing Together

▶ ## Large Group Activity: Story and Dance

Note: This story incorporates a simplified version of Mary's Song of Praise, the Magnificat. Simple dance movements are suggested (in italics) to go with the words. Ask several participants before the session to learn these slow, dramatic movements to teach to the rest of your parish family.

Mary had traveled a long way from her home in Nazareth to see her cousin Elizabeth and her cousin's husband, Zechariah. Mary loved them very much, and the three of them always enjoyed being together.

Mary was especially fond of Elizabeth and had been sad for her because Mary knew how much Elizabeth had always wanted a child of her own. But Elizabeth had given up hope of ever having a baby. "I'm just too old now," Elizabeth had said to Mary about a year before.

Then only a few days ago, God's angel Gabriel had told Mary that not only would she herself have a baby, but that Elizabeth was six months pregnant! Mary was eager to visit Elizabeth so that they could talk with each other about what was happening to them. They were both going to have babies!

As Mary walked up to the front door of Zechariah and Elizabeth's house, she was practically dancing. She let herself into the inner courtyard.

"Elizabeth! Elizabeth!" she called. "It's Mary!"

At that very moment, Elizabeth's baby moved inside her, and suddenly Elizabeth knew how special Mary's baby would be.

Elizabeth called out to Mary, "You are the most blessed of all women! And blessed is the child you will bear! The mother of God's own son is visiting me! As soon as I heard you call out to me, the baby within me jumped with gladness."

Mary was indeed happy to be chosen to be the mother of the baby Jesus. And she shared with Elizabeth a song of praise from her heart:

The Magnificat (simplified)
My heart praises the Lord,
My soul is glad because of God my
    Savior.

For God has remembered me, God's humble servant! From now on all people will call me blessed, because of the great things the Mighty One has done for me. Holy is the name of God, who shows mercy to all who honor the Lord.

Begin with all dancers grouped together looking inward. One steps forward and crosses her hands over her heart, raises her arms in praise, then kneels with folded hands as the other dancers place their hands on her head.

Then all bow down.

God has stretched out a mighty arm

Dancers raise and stretch their arms as though encircling the world.

and scattered the proud people with all their plans.

All make a slow, dramatic side to side sweeping motion.

God brought down mighty kings from their thrones, and lifted up the lowly.

All reach their arms far upward, then bend all the way down as though placing something on the floor. Dancers reverse the last motion.

God has filled the hungry with good things

All pretend to pass food to the children in the audience.

and sent the rich away with empty hands.

All dancers turn away from the audience and walk with outstretched hands.

God kept the promise made to our grandparents.

All join hands and walk in a circle.

God came to help us and remembered to show mercy to all of us forever!

The dancers form a group, some standing and others kneeling. Raise hands in praise.

Mary and Elizabeth hugged each other and laughed and cried and prayed and shared secrets and talked and talked and talked. Mary stayed with Elizabeth and Zechariah for almost three months; then Mary went back home to Nazareth.

She and Joseph had much to do before Mary's own special baby was to be born. But she would never forget this precious time with her cousin Elizabeth.

Small Group Activity: Word Search

Materials

copies of the puzzle below
pens or pencils
Bibles

You might want to form small groups for this activity, including all ages in each group. Adults can help young children recount the story by asking questions about the characters. Elementary age and older children can work on the puzzle below:

ZECHARIAH
ELIZABETH
JOHN
GABRIEL
MARY
JOSEPH
SHEPHERDS
JESUS
SIMEON
ANNA

Do you know what part these people played in the story of Jesus' birth? Circle their names—hidden in a vertical or horizontal line—in the puzzle below. Then in the space beside each name above, write what part the person played in the nativity story. If you need help, you can find their stories in Luke 1:26-45, 57-66 and 2:4-15, 21-38.

```
S  I  M  A  R  J  E  S  U  S
H  Z  E  C  H  A  R  I  A  H
I  E  L  I  Z  O  N  M  N  E
S  H  I  M  O  J  S  E  S  P
J  O  Z  M  C  O  U  O  G  H
F  Q  A  A  K  S  X  N  A  E
G  A  B  T  I  E  L  O  B  R
W  N  E  Y  M  P  A  N  B  D
J  N  T  J  O  H  N  E  L  S
O  A  H  N  N  D  S  G  X  A
```

▶ Small Group Activity: Christmas Card Puppets

Materials

    assortment of old Christmas cards
    tongue depressors or strips of cardboard
    glue
    scissors
    Bible

Invite participants to make a set of stick puppets to use in dramatizing the Christmas story. Ask the participants to cut out nativity figures from old Christmas cards, and glue the figures to tongue depressors or strips of cardboard.

Ask the participants to use their finished figures to act out the story you read or tell in your own words—from Luke 2:1-20.

Leader's Resources: Multicultural Issues

● What aspects of Advent celebrations from other countries can you include in this session? Consider the celebration of Simbang Gabi from the Philippines, which takes place on nine days close to Christmas, with special prayers, liturgies and gatherings. Las Posadas, from Mexico, re-enact the journey of Mary and Joseph to Bethlehem. (The Christmas card puppet activity could be adapted for a play for Las Posadas.)

● The celebration of Our Lady of Guadalupe on December 12 offers an occasion to explore Hispanic activities and music. Consider praying the Hail Mary in Spanish, or singing one of the popular Guadalupe songs, such as "Viva La Virgen De Guadalupe," from *Canticos* (OCP, Portland, OR). You can also show the video *Our Lady of Guadalupe*, available in English or Spanish from St. Anthony Messenger Press and Franciscan Communications (Cincinnati, OH).

● For children, read aloud *The Legend of the Poinsettia* by Tomie de Paola. This lovely Mexican legend connects the blooming of the poinsettia, "La Flor de Nochebuena" (flower of the Holy Night) with the humble gift of a young girl.

● Another song in Spanish for this season is the well-known "Digo Si, Señor" (reminiscent of the "Magnificat") by Donna Pena (GIA, Chicago, IL).

● Are families within your church also preparing to observe Kwanzaa? Invite them to share their preparations with participants.

Key Idea

Advent is a time when we prepare our hearts, that Jesus may be born in us. Thus, Advent is both a time of joyful preparation and repentance.

Large Group Activity: Advent Wreaths

The Advent wreath is a tradition that helps us take time out from our busy Christmas preparations to open our hearts to Jesus. (There is a picture of one at the beginning of this chapter.)

The circular form of the wreath, like God's love, is never-ending. The greenery that covers it reminds us of everlasting life and hope because evergreen trees are green even in the midst of winter.

The candles are symbols of the light God brings us. Three of them are purple, the royal color for the new King. The fourth candle is pink and is lit on the Third Sunday of Advent when we celebrate with special joy. Some people light a white candle, the Christ candle, in the center of the wreath on Christmas Day.

At your parish family session, invite participants to make Advent wreaths to symbolize the everlasting nature of God's love and light. You can offer several methods by setting up materials for each method at separate tables. Invite families to work together to make an Advent wreath for their homes.

Method One:

Materials

heavy and light weight florist's wire
evergreens
4 short candle holders for each wreath
3 purple candles and 1 rose candle for each wreath

Optional:
florist's or modeling clay
purple ribbon
sprays of berries
pine cones

Bend the heavy wire into a circle 12" in diameter. (To make the wreath sturdier and fuller, you might choose to make a second, smaller circle, place it within the first, and wire the two together with short lengths of wire.)

Trim the circular form with evergreens, bound to it with lightweight wire. Place the wreath where you will be using it and put four short candle holders at equal distance around the circle.

If necessary, use bits of modeling or florist's clay to hold the candles securely in the candle holders. Add a purple bow, berries or pine cones, if desired, for decoration.

Method Two:

Materials

1 dinner plate for each wreath (ask each family to bring a plate from home)

florist's clay

3 purple candles and 1 rose candle for each wreath

lightweight florist's wire

evergreens

Optional:

1 white candle for each wreath

purple ribbon

sprays of berries

pine cones

Use florist's clay to secure the three purple and one pink candles to the dinner plate. (Add one white candle in the center to represent Christ, if desired.)

Use lightweight florist's wire to bind small bundles of greenery and place these on the plate to form the wreath. Add a purple bow, berries or pine cones to decorate the wreath, if desired.

Method Three:

Materials

1" to 1-1/2" thick cross sections of a log 10"-12" in diameter

drill with 1/2" bit

3 purple candles and 1 rose candle for each wreath

staple gun and staples

evergreens

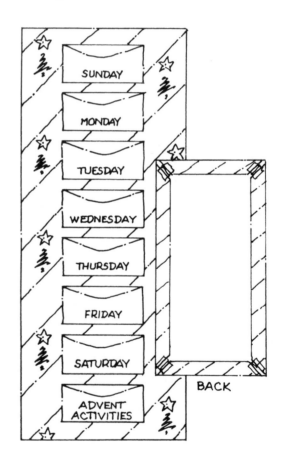

Drill four or five 1/2" deep holes in each cross section of log. Place one candle in each hole. Use the staple gun to attach evergreens to the wood.

You can find a prayer for the "Blessing of an Advent Wreath" on pages 110-112 of *Catholic Household Blessings and Prayers*, and prayers that include lighting the candles in "At Table During Advent" on pages 64-69.

Small Group Activity: Advent Calendars

Materials

glue
envelopes
burlap or poster board (any color)
   or green poster board and scissors
pens or pencils
3" x 5" memo pads
Optional:
Christmas gift wrap
scissors
clear tape

Invite participants to make Advent calendars as gifts for the other participants. Form groups of three or four people each.

Ask each group to glue eight envelopes down the length of a strip of burlap or poster board. If desired, first cover one side of the poster board with Christmas gift wrap, folding it over the edges of the poster board, and taping the gift wrap in place. Or use green poster board and cut it in the shape of a large Christmas tree,

making sure that all eight envelopes will fit on it.

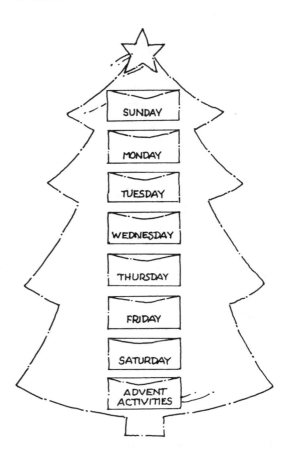

Write the name of each weekday on an envelope. Mark the eighth envelope with the words Advent Activities.

Ask the participants to brainstorm activities appropriate for Advent, such as:
● add a figure to your creche
● make a Christmas card for a friend
● read Mary's song in Luke 1:46-55
● give coins to a Salvation Army kettle
● sing an Advent song
● make a present for Jesus.

Growing Together

Ask the participants to write the activities on slips of memo paper, using one slip for each activity, and providing one activity for each day of Advent. Put all the slips in the envelope marked Advent Activities.

Invite the groups to make enough calendars so that each person present will receive one. Put all the calendars from all the groups together, then ask one or two children to distribute one to each person.

Directions to recipients: Post your calendar on your wall. Each Sunday during Advent, take seven slips of paper from the Advent Activities envelope on your calendar. Put one slip in each of the other envelopes. Each day pull a slip out of the appropriate envelope and follow its instructions.

Key Idea

How can everything we do to prepare for Christmas ready us to welcome God's Gift? Jesus commanded, "Love others as I have loved you." What gifts will we give that express love like Jesus' love?

Small Group Activity: Christmas Ornaments

Materials

> small, gold metallic paper doilies
> glue
> old Christmas cards
> thread (gold, if possible)
> scissors

Make a simple Christmas tree ornament by gluing two gold metallic doilies together, shiny sides out. Cut a small nativity story figure out of an old Christmas card and glue the figure in the center of one of the doilies. String gold thread through the top of the ornament as a hanger. (One of these could be tucked in with a Christmas card to a friend.)

Small Group Activity: Gift Wrap

Materials

> butcher paper or shelf paper
> pages from the classified section of a
>   newspaper
> objects for printing: cookie cutters;
>   empty spools; jar lids; square rubber

erasers; sponges cut into the shapes
of stars, trees, angels, etc.
thick red and green tempera paint
cookie sheets or disposable pie pans
paper towels

Make a stamp pad for printing by putting
10 or so paper towels on a cookie sheet
or in a pie pan and saturating the paper
towels with thick red or green paint. Make
enough stamp pads to scatter these around
your work tables.

Give each participant a 3-foot length of
paper or a page of newspaper. Invite
everyone to make wrapping paper by dip-
ping various objects into paint and press-
ing the objects onto the paper. Repeated
designs are especially effective.

Small Group Activity:
Birthday Cards for Jesus

Materials

4-1/2" x 12" strips of construction paper,
1 per person
scissors
construction paper in assorted colors
glue
felt pens

Show how to fold a strip of paper in an
accordion fold, so that each folded section
is 3" wide. Tell the participants that since
Christmas is Jesus' birthday, your parish
family will make pictures of gifts to give
Jesus.

Ask each participant to think of three gifts
for Jesus, to make pictures of the gifts

from construction paper, and to glue one
picture on each section of the birthday
card. Ask participants to write birthday
messages to Jesus on the cards, as well.

Small Group Activity:
Discussion
(for older participants)

Materials

paper
pens or pencils

Ask each participant to make a list of special Christmas memories, to pick one of
the best, and write its story with as many
details as possible. Allow 10-15 minutes.

Next ask each participant to list all the elements that made that memory special.
Suggest such elements as:
food
presents
one special gift
family
friends
music
prayer
house decorations
weather
place
church service

Ask participants to circle the three most
important elements on the list. Allow 10
minutes for this activity.

Divide the group into small groups of four
or five members each to discuss these
questions:

Growing Together

- What are the most important elements of our favorite Christmas memories?
- What elements of our Christmas observances do we spend the most time or money on today?
- What do we want more of in our observances? What do we want less of in our observances?
- How can we make these changes?

 ## Leader's Tip

An excellent resource to use in exploring simpler Christmas celebrations is *Unplug the Christmas Machine: A Complete Guide to Putting Love and Joy Back into the Season* by Jo Robinson and Jean Stacheli (New York, Quill, 1991).

Large Group Activity: Quiet Time/Festive Time

Materials

evergreen boughs

5 or 6 candles in holders

audio tape and player or musicians from your parish family to play Christmas hymns

prepared slips of paper in basket

5 or 6 pictures of situations or places in our world where there is poverty, violence or other tragedy

craft supplies (paper and fabric scraps, cardboard tubes, pipe cleaners, aluminum foil, modeling clay, cotton balls, etc.)

small natural objects (pine cones, twigs, rocks, etc.)

This is not so much a single activity as a plan for an evening for adults and older children, combining the penitence and joy of Advent. The first part of the evening is silent, except for music. Ideally a large, open room with a rug works best, so that people are comfortable sitting on the floor.

Tell people in advance that the first part of the evening will be a time for reflection and the second part will be a party. Ask everyone to bring food and drink to share at the party. (You might want to plan an event for young children on the same evening and invite them in to join the party.)

Post signs asking everyone to enter silently. Maintain this silence until everyone has gathered. Before participants arrive, set up five or six places around the room where people will pray. At each of these, have a lighted candle on the floor. Encircle the candle with evergreen boughs and a picture that shows people or situations that need God's healing love.

Set the craft supplies, including the small natural objects, on a table. When everyone has gathered, explain that you will pass a basket with slips of paper.

On each slip is written the name of one of the figures in the nativity story. Ask each person to draw a slip, choose craft supplies and find a corner in which to create a figure representing the name on the slip.

Maintain silence while everyone works. Each participant is to think about why this particular figure happened to be the one he or she drew. Or to put it another way, Why did this figure choose you?

Directions to participants: After you make your figure, go and place it near one of the candles. Stop there to meditate briefly on what the picture may suggest to you. Ask God what needs to be born in you this Christmas.

Continue: Go and meditate briefly at each candle, then place your figure in the center of our room where our creche will be.

Choose an appropriate Christmas hymn to sing together, gathered around the creche. Then greet each other with the phrase, "Blessed birth."

Now begin your party!

Closing Prayer

Here are several options to choose from:
- If you used the Jesse Tree activities, **before the session**, write on a separate slip of paper the name of each of the biblical people in the Jesse Tree books. Give each person a slip, until all the strips are distributed.
  Tell children who cannot read yet what their slips say. If chronological order is important to you, seat everyone in correct sequence. Ask each person to offer, in his or her own words, thanks to God for the person named on the slip. The person who has the slip with "you" written on it closes the prayer by giving thanks for all members of God's family.
- Close by reading again the Magnificat and doing the movement activity together.
- Close with a proclamation of one of the Sunday lectionary readings from the season of Advent.
- Close with a few moments of silence preceded by these thoughts: Dear God, we fill our days with busy things; things that are necessary and things that are not. Take these precious moments of quiet we offer back to you now, and fill us with what you know we need. *(Silence)* Thank you, God.

Christmas

Introduction and Information

Our Christmas liturgy is drawn from two ancient traditions, that of the Eastern Church and that of the Western Church. The Eastern Church's incarnational liturgy emphasized the manifestation of God in Jesus, making Epiphany the chief incarnational feast.

This emphasis marks the lectionary for Christmas Day. The second reading praises God's Son, who "reflects the brightness of God's glory and is the exact likeness of God's own being" (Heb. 1:3). The gospel, from John, ends with a witness to Jesus' glory, "received as the Father's only Son" (Jn. 1:14).

The Western Church's incarnational liturgy emphasized the humble birth of Jesus at Bethlehem, making Christmas, December 25, the chief incarnational feast. The Church picked this date to coincide with a pagan festival celebrating the return of light at the winter solstice. Hence, the opening prayer for Mass at Midnight praises God for making "this holy night radiant with the splendor of Jesus Christ...the true light of the world."

Western culture—from the most sophisticated art to the humblest folk custom—has retained this Christmas focus on the birth at Bethlehem. This focus has given rise to many traditions such as Christmas lullabies, nativity pageants and the creche.

A Feast and a Season

The Church gives us time to enjoy all these traditions by making Christmas not only a day, but a season. Christmas season begins with first vespers of Christmas and ends with the feast of the Baptism of the Lord on the Sunday after Epiphany. The full observance of the Christmas season, and the preservation of our traditions, can help us keep the Christmas celebrations of our families and parishes centered on Jesus.

The season is enriched by one feast after another. Christmas Day is followed by the feast of the Holy Family on the first Sunday after Christmas and the Solemnity of Mary, Mother of God on January 1. The gospel for the day tells how Mary treasured in her heart all that was said about her Son, who was given the name of Jesus on the eighth day of his birth. January 1 is also the civil New Year, which can serve to remind us that God's salvation redeems all time.

Growing Together

Come and Worship

For this is the season of our salvation, and the birth of our Redeemer. Come and worship the Son who reveals the glory of his Father. Come and worship the Child born in a humble stable at Bethlehem.

Come and worship the Son of Mary and Joseph, the King who comes as a Servant. Come and worship him who shares our life in family, our life alone.

Come and worship him whose name is the sign of our salvation, even Jesus Christ our Lord.

Note: This chapter provides two kinds of activities to sustain the Christmas celebration for the full season. Most of the activities are designed for use at a parish family session; others are designed for use on specific days, such as the feast of the Holy Family or the Solemnity of Mary, Mother of God.

Help! How do I plan this session?

How will I publicize this session?

_____

_____

How many people do I think might participate? _____

What are the ages of the participants?

_____

Where will we hold the session?

_____

Which recommended activities would work best with this particular group of participants? (Remember, we provide more activities than most groups can use in a single session. Pick a few that will work for your group.)

_____

_____

_____

_____

_____

_____

_____

_____

Volunteers

to do	names	phone numbers
planning:		
preparation and set-up:		
activity leaders:		
clean-up:		

Session Plan

Gathering Prayer

Invite participants to sing together a beloved Christmas carol.

Key Idea

Parish celebrations help focus our Christmas joy on the revelation of God in Jesus Christ.

Small Group Activity: Seeing Jesus, Knowing God

Materials

    old shirts
    sheets of finger-paint paper
    finger paint
    sponges
    water

Have old shirts available to protect participants' clothing. Ask each participant to fold a sheet of finger-paint paper as if closing a book. Invite participants to open the papers, dab on water with a sponge, and spread finger paint on the right-hand half of each sheet.

Ask the participants to draw pictures or symbols in the paint to represent Jesus. Encourage younger participants to simply draw pictures of Jesus. Encourage older participants to invent pictures or symbols that show Jesus as the participants know him, as Teacher or Healer or Mystery. Encourage all participants to use simple, bold lines.

Help a participant who is finished drawing close the paper carefully on the fold, then reopen it. The picture of Jesus will leave a mirror image on the left-hand half of the paper. Help young participants label the right-hand side of the pictures with the name *Jesus*, and the left-hand side with the name *God*.

Discuss these questions with older participants:
- How do you perceive Jesus in the gospels?
- What qualities describe Jesus?
- What roles describe Jesus?
- What evidence do we have from scripture that these qualities and roles describe God?
- What evidence do we have from experience that these qualities and roles describe God?

Close by reading to the group John 1:18, "No one has ever seen God. The only Son, who is the same as God and is at the Father's side, he has made him known."

Story: Emmanuel, God with Us

God called the angels together and they crowded about, leaning forward with excitement to hear the news.

God spoke: "This day my Son, Jesus, has been born in Bethlehem. He will show all people how deeply I love them. They will learn from him what it is like to be with me. They will even call him *Emmanuel*— God with us.

"Go now, angels! Not one, not two, not three of you, but all of you! Go and tell the good news. Tell the news to the shepherds taking care of their sheep in fields near Bethlehem. Tell the news to kings who live far away."

Off the angels flew to sing a new song of good news: "A child is born. His name is Jesus and he is God's Son. Glory to God in the highest, and peace to God's people on earth."

As the angels sang, a new star appeared in the sky. It came to rest right over the stable in Bethlehem where Jesus, Mary and Joseph were staying.

The shepherds who were taking care of their sheep in the fields nearby were amazed and frightened at the brightness of the star. But then they saw an angel. Can you imagine how they trembled?

The angel said to them, "Don't be afraid, for I bring you good news of great joy. To you this very day in Bethlehem, a Child— a Savior—has been born. He is Christ the Lord. You will know this Child when you find a newborn Baby wrapped in strips of cloth and lying in a manger."

Suddenly the shepherds saw not just one angel, but thousands of angels, all the host of heaven. The angels were singing, "Glory to God in the highest and peace to God's people on earth."

When the angels left, the shepherds said to one another, "Let's go into Bethlehem right now and look for this baby. Just imagine, angels came to tell *us!* Why, we may be the first to know! Us! Just simple shepherds. Let's run! Hurry! See the bright star? It hangs there low in the sky. Follow it. Hurry! Hurry!"

Away the shepherds ran, as fast as they could go. They found the stable where Mary and Joseph were. They found Jesus lying in a manger, wrapped in swaddling clothes, just as the angel had told them. This was the Baby. This was the Savior!

Growing Together

"We came to see the Baby," the shepherds said.

"His name is Jesus," Joseph whispered to the shepherds.

"How did you know about him?" Mary asked.

"How did you know to look here?" Joseph asked.

The shepherds told Mary and Joseph all they had heard and seen, about the sky full of angels and the new, bright star. One of the shepherds said to Joseph, "The angels said 'to *you* a child has been born.' What can that mean? Could it mean that this Baby, this Savior, came to show *you* and *me* God's love?"

The shepherd smiled and looked shyly at Joseph. "You know," he said, "if Jesus were born into my family, this is just the kind of place he would be born. My children came into the world on our farm, and there were more animals around than people! Why, Jesus even looks a lot like my youngest did. But there's something special about this child, isn't there?"

Joseph smiled and placed his hand on the shepherd's shoulder. "Yes," Joseph said, "there is. This Baby is God's Son. There is more to his birth than even his mother and I understand. But rejoice and celebrate with us, because this child will save his people."

Joseph, Mary and the shepherds smiled at the Baby sleeping in the manger. Their hearts and voices sang grateful songs of praise to God. The angels in heaven rejoiced because God's plan was being carried out in this simple place with these simple people.

"Hallelujah! To all of us a Child is born! Hallelujah! Hallelujah!"

▶ Large Group Activity: Surprise Party

Materials

    birthday cake in a box or container
    birthday candles
    cans or bottles of juice or soft drinks
    party paper goods: napkins, plates,
       cups, plastic forks
    gift wrap
    hamper, basket or box

Before the session wrap the napkins, cups, plates, candles, etc., in enough packages so that each child in the group will have at least one to open. Wrap the cake in a container. Bring the packages to the session in a basket, hamper or box.

At the session give each child a package to open. You may wish to hand out the packages one at a time.

Save the cake package for last. If the participants have not guessed by now, announce a birthday party for Jesus. Ask everyone to help set a table and put candles in the cake. When everything is ready, light the candles. Invite the participants to sing *Happy Birthday to Jesus,* blow out the candles and enjoy the party.

100

Key Idea

The Christmas creche helps us focus our Christmas celebration on the birth of Jesus in Bethlehem.

Large Group Activity: Creche Sharing

Materials

> parish creche
> family creches

Before the session find long-standing members of the parish who know the history of the parish creche. Ask these people to prepare a short talk on that history to present at the parish family session. These "elders" might also describe the celebration of Christmas before the changes in the Catholic Church begun by the Second Vatican Council.

Invite participants to bring their creches to the session, too.

At the session have the participants arrange their creches in a display, and encourage everyone to share stories about the creches. Invite the participants to visit the parish creche to hear a special story from parish history.

Small Group Activity: What's Missing Game

Materials

> creche with figures

This game is especially appropriate if the group includes young children. Ask participants to close their eyes. Remove one figure from the creche. Ask participants to open their eyes and guess which figure is missing. Let one of the participants be the next person to remove a figure.

This game can be simplified for preschoolers by limiting the number of figures to three or four. Ways to *increase* the game's difficulty include:
- using more items
- rearranging the items before removing one
- removing more than one item
- rearranging the items without removing any.

Small Group Activity: Shoe Box Creches

Materials

> 2 cups baking soda
> 1 cup cornstarch
> saucepan
> 1-1/2 cups water
> wooden spoon
> measuring cup
> cookie sheet
> food coloring
> storage containers
> shoe boxes, 1 for each participating
> household

Growing Together

cardboard

scissors

glue

dried pine needles or excelsior or
    shredded paper

Before the session make cornstarch clay
in this way: Mix together the baking soda
and the cornstarch in a saucepan. Slowly
stir in 1 to 1-1/2 cups of cold water, until
the mixture is smooth. Cook over moder-
ate heat, stirring constantly (or it will burn)
until the mixture is stiff. Turn onto a
cookie sheet and cool.

When the dough is cool, knead it until it is
pliable. Tint some of it with food coloring,
leaving a small amount plain. Store each
color of dough in a separate container or
plastic bag. This recipe makes enough
cornstarch clay for about 1-3 creches.

At the session show the participants how
to make figures—of Mary, Joseph, the
baby or the animals—by pulling ap-
pendages *out* of a single piece of clay.
(Some people may want to make shepherds and an angel, too.) Invite each
household to make one creche.

Use a shoe box as a stable for each
creche. Mangers and troughs may be cut
from cardboard. Pine needles can be used
for straw on the floor.

Leader's Tip

The cornstarch clay may be left
untinted. Instead, you can air dry the
items before painting them with ordinary tempera paints. This technique is
appropriate for ongoing religious education settings, where children can
make the clay objects one week and
paint them the next.

Key Idea

Parish festivities extend the celebration of Christmas through all
12 days, giving full expression to
the joy of God's people in the
birth of God's child.

▶ **Large Group Activity:
Caroling**

Materials

song books (one choice would be the "Breaking Bread" song book from OCP, Portland, OR)

Invite participants to go caroling in the neighborhood surrounding the parish. You can use parish music resources or other appropriate songbooks, or simply encourage participants to choose several well-known carols.

This project could be extended over time. Consider learning carols together in Advent, and ending with a caroling walk during Christmas season.

▶ **Small Group Activity:
On-the-Spot Pageant**

Materials

books or booklets of Christmas carols
Bible
Optional:
makeshift costumes

Hold an impromptu Christmas pageant by inviting participants to act out with silent movements the Christmas story, as it is read. Ask one group of participants to be the chorus. Give these participants song books and a list of the carols to be practiced.

Ask the other participants to choose parts from this list:

narrator (only speaking part)

Mary
Joseph
animals in manger
shepherds
angels

Ask these participants to practice their movements as the narrator reads.

To perform the pageant, bring the two groups together, and alternate readings as follows:

reading: Luke 2:1-4
carol: "O, Little Town of Bethlehem"

reading: Luke 2:5-7
carol: "Silent Night, Holy Night"

reading: Luke 2:8-14
carol: "Go, Tell It On the Mountain"

reading: Luke 2:15-20
carol: "O Come, All Ye Faithful" (Older generations might appreciate the chance to sing the traditional Latin version, too: "Adeste Fideles")

▶ **Large Group Activity:
Christmas Party**

Invite the parish family to an old-fashioned Christmas party—perhaps even a masquerade.

Here are some suggestions for party activities.

Growing Together

Recipe: Wassail Punch

Materials

1 gallon apple cider
2 cinnamon sticks
1 whole nutmeg
5-6 whole cloves
stainless steel or enameled pot, at least
6 quart capacity

Put all the ingredients in a pot. Bring to a simmer, but do not boil. Simmer for 30 minutes. Serve warm.

Large Group Activity: Folk Dances

Find members of the parish who can teach folk dances to the other participants. One parish alternates between Greek circle dances and country swing on holidays!

Small Group Activity: Put the Star on the Tree

Materials

3' tree cut from green construction
paper
masking tape
3" stars cut from yellow construction
paper
blindfold
felt pen

Tape the tree to a wall of the room. Put a loop of masking tape on the back of each star. Invite everyone to play Put the Star on the Tree.

Blindfold one player at a time and give the player a star. Turn the player around in a slow circle twice, then give a gentle push in the right direction.

Ask the player to walk to the wall and touch it. When the player touches the wall, he or she must stick the star on the exact spot touched. Let the player remove the blindfold, and write his or her name on the star.

Repeat until everyone has had a turn. The winner is the one to stick a star closest to the top of the tree.

Large Group Activity: Giving Tree

Materials

donations
boxes
wrapping paper
ribbons
cards

If a Giving Tree was used in Advent (p. 75) you might ask participants to bring their donations to the party. Set up a table where participants can wrap the donations. For ways to print your own wrapping paper, see page 90. (Make sure participants clearly mark the organizations for whom the donations are intended.)

Stack the wrapped presents under the parish Christmas tree, or at the parish creche, as presents for Jesus.

Key Idea

On the first Sunday after Christmas, we celebrate the Holy Family. In our own households, as well as in our parish family, we strive to imitate the ideals of love, witness and servant ministry that characterized the lives of Jesus, Mary and Joseph.

Large Group Activity: Caroling to Shut-Ins

See above for caroling ideas. Invite carolers to include parish shut-ins in their visits. Consider also visits to such community institutions as nursing homes, crisis shelters and halfway houses.

Large Group Activity: Feeding the Hungry

Invite participants to offer time today to serve food to the hungry. If the parish has no such ongoing ministry of its own, contact organizations in the community that do. Plan to include children in this project.

Large Group Activity: Parish Work Day

Invite participants to spend time together ministering to the needs of the parish's building. Compile a list of maintenance or clean-up jobs that need to be done in the building, being sure to include small jobs that children can tackle with success. Provide refreshments, and plan extra time for singing, games or Mass at the end of the work session.

Large Group Activity: Holy Family Frontal

Materials

Bibles
5 12" x 18" felt rectangles, in assorted colors
yarn in assorted colors
fabric scraps
beads
buttons
scissors
glue
white bed sheet
pencil

Note: If preferred, this activity could be adapted by having groups design small symbols, for the Holy Family or for Christmas, to be attached to the priest's chasuble for a children's Mass.

Divide the group of participants into five groups. Assign one of the short Bible passages below to each group. (Each passage tells a short story about the Holy Family.) Passages:

Matthew 1:18-24
Matthew 2:13-15, 19-23
Luke 2:15-21
Luke 2:22-40
Luke 2:41-51

Growing Together

Give each group a felt rectangle. Ask each group to create a design for its assigned Bible story, making the design large enough to fill the rectangle. For example, group one might construct a design symbolizing Joseph's dream, or Joseph's protective care of his family.

The groups can use one of two techniques: 1) collage (assembling the image from yarn, fabric, beads, buttons, etc., and gluing these to the rectangle); or 2) making shapes of yarn and filling in each shape with a winding, concentric pattern of yarn.

As the groups work, drape the sheet over the parish altar. Use a pencil to mark the edges of the part of the sheet that will be visible on the front of the altar.

Invite a participant with a good eye for design to orchestrate the groups as they glue the constructed symbols within the marked edges of the frontal. Use the frontal on the altar during a Mass in honor of the Holy Family.

▶ Large Group Activity: Children's Day

Some European countries traditionally observed a *Children's Day* on December 28, the day when the Holy Innocents were remembered and honored. Children were put in charge of the day's activities at home or at school.

Consider adapting this Christmas custom by letting the parish youth group plan activities for Holy Family, or by holding a children's day party at which children are the guests of honor, and are given the starring roles in games and activities.

Leader's Resources: Outreach

- Visits to shut-ins, bringing gifts and food treats, caroling would be seasonally appropriate outreach activities for families. Almost all parishes bring Eucharist to the home-bound through Eucharistic Ministers. Perhaps these ministers could occasionally be accompanied during the Christmas season by families bearing gifts.

- Encourage families to invite single or older members of the parish to their home for Christmas Day or on the Feast of the Holy Family.

- At the session, take up a "special collection" to send as a Christmas gift to an organization such as Food for the Poor to assist in disaster relief. As an alternative, designate the money for the parish food pantry or outreach programs for the homeless. Consider a presentation to families about such programs as "Save the Children Fund."

Key Idea

We celebrate the Solemnity of Mary, Mother of God on January 1. Scripture tells us this day is also the day when Jesus received his name. In honor of Mary and Jesus, our celebrations often include prayers for peace.

Small Group Activity: Name Banners

Materials

4 36" dowels, 1/2" thick

2 rectangles of burlap, each 30" x 60"

glue

felt or other fabric

trimmings, braid, rick-rack, piping, cording, sequins, beads, etc.

scissors

twine

Bibles, missals and prayer books

chalkboard or newsprint

Note: Several traditional symbols are pictured on the next page.

Ask the participants to make two Name Banners, one in honor of Mary and one in honor of Mary's Son, Jesus. Ask each group to include names drawn from the Bible and traditional prayer. (Litanies and the prayers of the Mass are both rich in possibilities.)

Participants can also brainstorm a list of their own ideas for names to celebrate Mary and Jesus. Record all suggestions on chalkboard or newsprint.

When each group has compiled a list of new and traditional names, ask the groups to cut letters from fabric to make names to glue onto the burlap. Encourage younger participants to trim the letters with rick-rack, braid, sequins, etc.

Glue each 30" edge of burlap around a dowel. Ask participants to glue the names to the banners. Fasten twine to the ends of the top dowels to hang the two banners.

Small Group Activity: A World at Peace

Materials

chalkboard and chalk or newsprint and marker

roll of butcher paper or newsprint

tape or tacks

tempera paints

paint brushes in assorted widths, 1/2"-2" wide

Across the top of the chalkboard, newsprint or poster board write *A world at peace...*

Ask:
- What would a world at peace look like? *(Write all answers under the heading* looks like...*)*
- What would a world at peace sound like? *(Write all answers under the heading* sounds like...*)*

Traditional Symbols for the Names of Jesus

Chi Rho
(first two letters of Greek spelling of Christ)

Alpha and Omega
Revelation 1:8
and 22:13

INRI
Latin inscription on cross of Calvary (John 19:19) meaning "Jesus of Nazareth, King of the Jews"

Crown of Life
Psalm 24:7-10
Revelation 11:15

Chi Rho with Anchor
(a symbol of hope)
Titus 2:13

IHS
(monogram derived from first three letters in Greek spelling of "Jesus")
Matthew 1:21

Ichthus
(Greek letters spell fish and make a rebus "Jesus Christ, God's Son, Savior")

Agnus Dei Lamb of God with Banner of Victory
Revelation 5:12-14

Rising Sun
Malachi 4:2

Bright and Morning Star
Revelation 22:16

Star of David
Numbers 24:17
Revelation 22:16

Manger with Chi Rho
Luke 2:11-12

- What would a world at peace feel like? *(Write all answers under the heading* feels like...*)*
- What would a world at peace smell like? *(Write all answers under the heading* smells like...*)*
- What would a world at peace taste like? *(Write all answers under the heading* tastes like...*)*

Invite participants to paint together a mural of a world at peace. Play peaceful music as the participants paint; we recommend "Kanon" by Pachelbel or "Jesu, Joy of Man's Desiring" by Bach.

Leader's Resources: Multicultural Issues

- Participants can sing together a simple carol, such as "Silent Night," in as many languages as are represented in the group: German, Polish, Italian, Spanish, Japanese, etc.
- A song that can be sung in Spanish and Latin simultaneously or separately is "O Sanctissima" and "Oh, Santisima" (from *Canticos* songbook, p. 163, OCP, Portland, OR).
- Ethnic food for Christmas is especially popular, and no Christmas gathering would be complete without sharing it. Invite participants to bring food, recipes and stories about family celebrations from times past.
- For the Feast of the Holy Family, ask participants to create and share pictures of their ethnic and cultural family backgrounds: significant ancestors, places of

origins, where and when their families settled in the United States, etc.

Note: See ideas for Epiphany and the Baptism of the Lord in the Epiphany session, beginning on page 111.

Closing Prayer

- Close with this prayer: Thank you, God, for being a God of surprise! The world waited for a King—and you sent a baby. Thank you for the joyful surprises you send us. Help us to share your wonderful surprises with those who don't yet know you.
- Close with a few quiet moments for participants to choose their favorite name for Jesus. Let each participant say his or her chosen name. Thank God for sending our Savior.
- From the Sacramentary, use the Opening Prayers for Mass at Midnight (p. 40) or the Solemn Blessings for Christmas (p. 470).
- Lead a scriptural rosary, in which the joyful mysteries centered on Christmas and the Holy Family are told verse by verse.
- "Peace" is one of the primary themes of the Christmas season. Participants can say or sing the "Gloria," then reflect briefly on the phrase "...and peace to God's people on earth." End by exchanging with one another the sign of peace.

Epiphany

Introduction and Information

The word *Epiphany* means manifestation. The readings for Epiphany manifest, or reveal, the person and nature of Jesus.

The feast of Epiphany is celebrated between January 2 and January 8. The Eastern Church celebrates this feast on January 6, a date chosen in ancient times to counteract a pagan festival in Egypt that marked the winter solstice. The pagan festival used themes of *light*, *water* and *wine*. Making use of these same elements, the Eastern Church celebrates the revelation of Jesus Christ at his birth, marked by the *light* of the nativity star; at his baptism in *water;* and at Cana, where he changed water to *wine*.

The Western Church, which had begun to celebrate Christmas on December 25 in opposition to a pagan winter solstice in Rome, appropriated some, but not all, of the Eastern significance of Epiphany. In the West, celebration of Epiphany emphasized the visit of the magi, guided by the nativity star. This event came to be interpreted as the revelation of Jesus Christ to the Gentiles.

Scripture does not describe the number or race or mode of travel of the magi. The biblical emphasis is on the magi's three gifts: gold, frankincense and myrrh. These gifts reveal the royal, divine and sacrificial nature of the infant Jesus.

Many customs exist in European countries that give the day far more significance than in our own culture. Some countries use this day, rather than Christmas Day, as the time to exchange gifts. Other countries observe the day with "Star Carols" sung by a procession of singers, dressed as magi and carrying stars.

The Baptism of Jesus, observed on the first Sunday after Epiphany, is an important feast of the season. At his baptism, Jesus is revealed as the Son of God and sealed by God's Holy Spirit. After this feast, the Sundays of Ordinary Time, between Epiphany and Lent, reveal Jesus enacting his baptismal ministry of preaching, teaching and healing.

Our own baptisms share in this manifestation or revelation. At baptism, each of us stood revealed as God's own son or daughter, sealed with the Holy Spirit, and called to ministry and mission.

As we come to the end of the Christmas season, let us look with joy to our Savior, revealed by the star that shone at his birth, by the waters of his baptism and by the power of his ministry. See, the Lord goes forth to teach, to preach and to heal. Let us look—and then follow.

Growing Together

Help! How do I plan this session?

How will I publicize this session?

_____

_____

How many people do I think might participate? _____

What are the ages of the participants?

_____

Where will we hold the session?

_____

Which recommended activities would work best with this particular group of participants? (Remember, we provide more activities than most groups can use in a single session. Pick a few that will work for your group.)

_____

_____

_____

_____

_____

_____

_____

Volunteers

to do	names	phone numbers
planning:		
preparation and set-up:		
activity leaders:		
clean-up:		

Session Plan

Gathering Prayer

The gospel for Epiphany is from Matthew 2:1-12. Proclaim this gospel at the beginning of the session.

Key Idea

The feast of Epiphany emphasizes the visit of the magi to the infant Jesus.

Story:
The Visit of the Kings

When Jesus is born in Bethlehem, a star shines in the sky right over the stable. Three kings in far-away lands see that new star. They know it means that something very special has happened. So they set out on their camels to follow the star. They follow the star for many days and many miles.

When the three kings arrive in Jerusalem, they stop to talk to the king of that land. His name is Herod. He is not a very good king at all. In fact, he is mean and wicked.

Herod asks, "What are you doing in my country?"

The kings tell him, "We are here to worship a new-born king. We have seen his star in the sky."

Herod is not happy when he hears that a new king is born. He asks the three wise men to come back to him after they find the new king. He says he wants to worship the newborn king, too. (But he is not telling the truth!)

The star moves across the sky and the three kings follow it. The star leads them on to Bethlehem and stops at the place where Jesus and Mary and Joseph live. The three kings go to the door and knock. (How do you think Mary and Joseph feel when they see three kings standing at their door?)

The kings have special gifts for Jesus. They carry the gifts in and lay them down by Baby Jesus. The gifts are gold, sweet smelling incense and myrrh, used as perfume or medicine.

The kings "ooh" and "ahh" at the beautiful baby. They smile and hold out their fingers for Jesus to squeeze. They laugh and tickle the baby, and make him smile and laugh. (Have you ever seen people do this to babies?)

The kings say goodbye to the little family and start their long journey home. They set up camp that night not far from Bethlehem. They eat supper and fall fast asleep.

Growing Together

That night in a dream God talks to the three kings. He says, "Do not go back and tell wicked King Herod about Jesus. Go home another way. Herod is evil and he wants to hurt Jesus!"

The next morning the kings start home by a road that leads far, far away from King Herod's palace. They sing and laugh and give thanks to God for his gift of Jesus to the world.

Small Group Activity: Story-Round

Materials

> star-shaped Christmas tree ornament or
> star cut from cardboard

Review the story of the birth of Jesus and the visit of the magi by holding a Story Round. Ask participants to sit in a circle. Begin the story with a sentence or two, such as:

At that time, the emperor demanded that everyone go to his hometown to be counted so that the emperor could collect tax money from all of his people. Joseph and Mary traveled to Joseph's home city of Bethlehem, to be counted.

Hand the star to the next person in the circle, who continues the story by adding a sentence. Then that person passes the star to the next person in the circle, who continues the story and hands on the star.

Continue around the circle until the whole story has been told. This may be repeated with new groups of participants.

Small Group Activity: King's Game

Materials

> road map

Note: This game is especially suitable for young children.

Ask participants to sit in a circle. Choose one participant to be "It." Give "It" a folded road map. "It" walks around the outside of the circle as the group chants this rhyme:

We've followed the star a long, long way
We've followed the star a long, long way
We've followed the star a long, long way
How many miles will we travel today?
1-2-3-4-5, etc.

As the group says *today*, "It" drops the road map in the lap of the nearest player, and runs around the circle, trying to get to that player's place before the player with the road map tags "It." If "It" gets to the place, the participant with the road map becomes It, and the game continues. If "It" gets tagged, the same player continues to be "It."

Small Group Activity: Gifts for Jesus

Materials

Bible
paper
pens or pencils
felt pens
tape

Read, or tell in your own words, Matthew 2:1-12. Discuss:

- How did the magi try to find Jesus?
- How do we try to find Jesus?
- What gifts did the magi bring?
- What gifts can we bring?

Encourage participants to express respect for every answer. For example, if a child says "a skateboard" in answer to the last question, look the child directly in the eyes as you say, "You'd like to give Jesus a skateboard. I think Jesus would have fun playing with that!"

When participants have had a chance to express their ideas, ask everyone to write or draw presents to give to Jesus. If participants choose to share their work, you can mount the drawings and writings on a wall, in a formation shaped like a star.

Key Idea

Epiphany may be celebrated with such rich, festive traditions as a King's Cake and a procession of carolers carrying stars aloft.

Leader's Tip

Look in a children's library for a copy of *Old Befana* by Tomie de Paola. This colorful book is a charming version of an Italian folktale about Epiphany.

Large Group Activity: King's Cake

Materials

cake ingredients:
1/2 cup blanched almonds
1 cup sugar
6 tablespoons soft butter (save the wrapper)
1 teaspoon vanilla or almond extract
2 eggs, lightly beaten
2 tablespoons raisins or currants
2-1/4 cups flour
1-1/2 teaspoons baking powder
tools:
blender or food processor
bowl

spoon
cookie sheet
forks
Optional:
beans
dimes
thimbles

The Three Kings' Cake is a European tradition. The cake—usually a flat circle, more like a cookie than a cake—hides a bean or two, a doll or a clutch of tiny fortunes. The significance of the hidden fortune varies. A hidden dime might signify wealth in the coming year. The finders of two dry beans might become king and queen of the Epiphany party. In New Orleans, the finder of a hidden black bean must give a party for all the other guests.

Invite participants to make—and eat—a traditional King's Cake. Directions:

Grind the almonds with 1/4 cup sugar in a food processor or blender. Use a fork to mix the butter and sugar together in a bowl. Mix until the butter and sugar are thoroughly blended. Beat in the eggs (saving a tablespoon of egg to glaze the top) and the extract.

Sift together the flour and baking powder into the egg mixture. Stir in the sugar-almond mix, the raisins or currants and any fortunes—such as beans—desired.

Turn the dough onto a greased cookie sheet. (Use the paper wrapping from the butter to grease the sheet.) Pat the dough flat into a 1/2" thick circle.

Spread the reserved beaten egg on the top of the cake. Bake at 350° Fahrenheit for 20 minutes. This recipe will serve 12 people.

Note: You can also make copies of this recipe for families to use at home.

▶ Large Group Activity: Epiphany Crowns

Invite participants to wear crowns as they eat King's Cake or sing Star Carols. Use one or both of these methods.

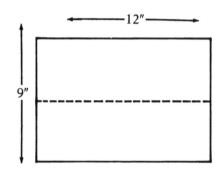

Construction-Paper Crowns

Materials

    9" x 12" construction paper in assorted colors
    scissors
    crayons
    felt pens
    glitter
    gummed stars
    glue
    clear tape or stapler

Simple construction-paper crowns may be made by cutting a 9" x 12" rectangle of construction paper in half lengthwise. The top edges of the paper may be cut into various shapes. (See diagram.)

Invite participants to decorate the crowns while flat, using materials such as glitter, crayons, felt pens, construction-paper shapes, gummed stars, etc.

Participants then glue, tape or staple the two ends of each crown together, being careful to check the fit first. (You will need two identical strips taped together to make a large enough crown.)

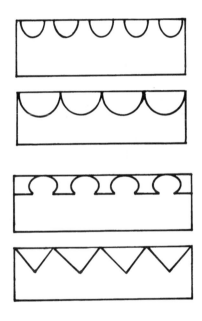

Star Hats

Materials
   12" x 18" metallic gift wrap paper in
      silver and gold
   scissors
   stapler
   construction paper
   glue

Each participant brings together the corners of a sheet of gold metallic paper and staples the paper to form a cone. Participants decorate the cone hats by cutting and pasting on silver star and moon shapes.

Large Group Activity: Star Carol Procession

Materials

   poles, dowels or sticks
   cardboard
   construction paper, preferably yellow
   glue
   scissors or a matte knife
   staple gun
   Optional:
   glitter, sequins, beads, etc.
   makeshift costumes
   songbooks

At one time, people in European countries could watch Epiphany plays performed by traveling groups of players. A vestige of this custom is retained in the Star Carol Procession, in which carolers go from place to place singing hymns appropriate to the season. The carolers carry poles topped by stars, to recall the star of Bethlehem, and sometimes dress in costumes, representing the magi and their entourage.

Invite participants to have a Star Carol Procession. Be sure to sing "We Three Kings of Orient Are" and "Go Tell It on the Mountain." Other songs suitable for Epiphany include:

Growing Together

- "All the Ends of the Earth" (Bob Dufford, SJ)
- "Here I Am, Lord" (Dan Shutte)
- "Seek the Lord" (Roc O'Connor, SJ)
- "Whatsoever You Do" (Willard Jabusch)
- "Sing Out, Earth and Skies" (Marty Haugen)

Provide poles, sticks or dowels for the star poles. Participants glue yellow construction paper over cardboard, then cut out stars. A matte knife will be easier to use than scissors, but keep the knife away from small children. Decorate the stars with glitter, sequins, streamers, etc.

Participants use a staple gun to attach the stars to the poles.

Note: *Catholic Household Blessings and Prayers* provides prayers for "Blessing of the Home and Household on the Epiphany" (p. 126-129)—another traditional custom.

Leader's Resources: Multicultural Issues

- Epiphany is a great time to bring together people from as many different ethnic and cultural backgrounds as possible. Enjoy sharing the diversity of food, music, stories, and, if appropriate, even ethnic dress.
- The magi brought gifts to Jesus. Participants at this session might discuss what gifts people of many countries and cultures have brought, whether to the

parish, to the community, to the country or to the Church.

- Catholicism is world-wide and "universal." Invite a panel of Catholics who have experienced life in the Church in other countries to talk about similarities and differences in their religious experience. Invite panelists to speak about their experiences in areas such as liturgy, religious education, sacramental symbols and celebrations and images of Jesus and God.

Key Idea

The Baptism of our Lord is the last feast of the Christmas season. After his baptism, Jesus enacts his calling through a ministry of preaching, teaching and healing.

Small Group Activity: Bible Study (for older participants)

Materials

copies of four Bible passages: Matthew 3:13-17, Mark 1:9-11, Luke 3:21-22 and John 1:29-34, 1 per participant
pens or pencils

Give each participant a set of copies of the four passages. Ask the participants to spend five minutes marking the passages to note differences and similarities.

Discuss:

● How are these passages similar?

— How do these passages differ?

— What would you choose as the most important emphasis of each passage? How could we outline the events of Jesus' baptism?

— Do these events have counterparts in our rites of baptism today?

— Do these events have counterparts in our daily lives as Christians?

Divide participants into small groups to discuss these questions:

● How would you define the mission of Jesus after his baptism?

— How would you define the mission of baptized Christians?

— How does this understanding of mission affect your daily life?

▶ Small Group Activity: Baptismal Calendars

Materials

chalkboard or newsprint

copies of a blank calendar for as many weeks as are needed for the Sundays between the Baptism of the Lord and Lent, 1 per participant

pens or pencils

Optional:

9" x 12" drawing paper
crayons or felt pens
scissors for children
glue or glue sticks

Invite participants to brainstorm ideas for a baptismal mission calendar. Ask participants to think of activities that carry out our baptismal mission. Record all ideas on chalkboard or newsprint.

Suggestions you may wish to add include:

● visit someone lonely today

● write a friendly note to another Christian today

● write a friendly note to a non-Christian today

● borrow some children's books from the library, and offer to read at the hospital today

● pray for world peace, and for troubled areas particularly

When the group has generated enough ideas, have each participant make a baptismal calendar to take home. Ask each participant to choose favorite activities, then write these on a blank calendar.

Encourage older participants to help younger ones with writing, as needed. Young children could make small drawings (using felt pens or crayons), cut the drawings out, and paste them onto their calendars while adults write in the activities that the children choose.

Growing Together

Large Group Activity: TV Special

Materials

Bibles

Divide the participants into three groups to prepare a mock TV Special on the Baptism of our Lord. Pass out Bibles to the participants, and ask them to use Matthew 3:13-17 as the basis of the TV Special.

Directions to the groups:

Group 1: Ask one member of the group to play the part of John the Baptist. Ask the other members to play reporters. Prepare questions and answers.

Group 2: Ask several members of the group to play the parts of bystanders. Ask the other members to play reporters. Prepare questions and answers.

Group 3: Ask one member of the group to play the part of Jesus. Ask the other members to play reporters. Prepare questions and answers.

Remind all the groups of the "five w's" of good reporting, *who*, *what*, *where*, *when* and *why*. Allow 10-15 minutes for planning, then reconvene the group. Participants present the interviews as a TV Special for the entire group.

Key Idea

Epiphany, the Baptism of the Lord and the weeks between these feasts and Lent all emphasize themes of outreach. The message of Jesus is for all people in all times and all places.

Small Group Activity: Bulletin Reflections (for older participants)

Materials

parish bulletins

Before the session consider inviting members of different parish organizations to attend the session and describe the work of their organizations.

At the session divide participants into small groups. Distribute bulletins. Invite each group to use the bulletins to discover how many activities exist in the parish that enact Jesus' ministry of peace and justice. Encourage participants to consider how they, too, enact that ministry as they discuss:

● In what ways do we support these activities now?
● In what ways do we want to support these activities in the future?

Small Group Activity: Epiphany Star

Materials

scissors

48" square of yellow felt

72" square of white cloth for background

glue

9" x 12" felt rectangles

felt scraps

trimmings, sequins, beads, rick-rack, etc.

Optional:

straight pins

Invite participants to make an Epiphany Star to symbolize the mission and ministry of Jesus. Plan to pin the finished star to the altar frontal or hang the star in a public part of the parish building.

At the parish family session, ask one participant to cut the 4' x 4' yellow square into two triangles. (Cut a diagonal line across the square to make the two triangles.) Overlap the triangles to make a six-pointed star. Glue the star onto the white background.

Divide the other participants into six groups. Ask each group to make one felt collage symbol to represent one of these stories. (Some of the stories suggested are traditional stories associated with the feast of Epiphany or the Baptism of the Lord. Others are drawn from the weeks of Ordinary Time preceding Lent.)

- visit of the magi
  reading: Matthew 2:1-12
  symbol: star or crown

- baptism of Jesus
  reading: Mark 1:9-11
  symbol: shell or dove
- wedding at Cana
  reading: John 2:1-11
  symbol: water jar or wine cup
- fishermen made disciples
  reading: Luke 5:1-11
  symbol: fish
- Jesus the teacher
  reading: Luke 8:16-21
  symbol: lamp
- Jesus the healer
  reading: Mark 1:29-34
  symbol: hands or flask of oil

Encourage each group to discuss its story. You may wish to have each group devise its own symbol, in order to encourage such discussion.

Growing Together

Each group cuts a 9" round from a 9" x 12" rectangle of felt. Each group then constructs its symbol, using this felt round for a background. Invite the participants to trim the symbols with shapes cut from felt scraps, beads, rick-rack, etc. Invite participants to work together to make a sign for Jesus.

Participants place the finished symbols on the Epiphany Star. Use straight pins, if necessary, to secure the symbols.

Leader's Resources: Outreach

- There's an old Epiphany saying that reads, "The wise still seek Him." Invite participants to consider what qualities it takes to seek God today. In what ways do believers still seek God?
- Remind and encourage participants to continue their support of agencies and programs that help the poor even though the holidays are coming to a close.
- Encourage families to invite a friend or neighbor to come with them to Mass.
- The beginning of the new year is a good time to make Epiphany resolutions and promises. Participants can take time to quietly determine how they could live Jesus' message of peace and justice in their own homes, in their neighborhoods and in the world. Invite participants to write down these "resolutions," sealing them in self-addressed stamped

envelopes. Leaders can hold the resolutions for a few weeks or months before mailing them back to the owners as reminders of their commitments.

Closing Prayer

Note: Consider the ages of the group's members when you choose one of these prayers or when the group offers its own spontaneous prayers.

- If you have planned a Star Carol procession, you might make it the last activity of the session. Singing Epiphany hymns, wind your way toward a creche that rests in some lovely corner of the parish building. Gather there, kneeling to pray.
- Or, if you made the Epiphany Star of felt, carry it in procession to the altar and pin it on the altar frontal. Invite each group to tell what its symbol represents and to give thanks for the good news revealed in that symbol.

Example: Our wine jar stands for the miracle at Cana when Jesus turned water into wine. We give thanks to you, Lord, that your power works miracles of transformation, not only long ago, but in our lives today.

- If the group includes many children, you may want to darken the room where you are meeting and shine a flashlight on the ceiling. Pray: Thank you, Jesus, that you are the light of the world. *(Then shine the light on each person, including yourself.)* Thank you, Jesus, that your light shines in each one of us. Show us how to share that light with others.

● End the service with the responsorial psalm for Epiphany, taken from Psalm 72. ("Lord, every nation on earth will adore you.")

Bibliography

Achtemeier, Paul J., gen. ed. *Harper's Bible Dictionary*. San Francisco: Harper and Row, 1985.

Ball, Peter. *Adult Believing*. New York: Paulist Press, 1988.

Beasley, James R., Clyde E. Fant, E. Earl Joiner, Donald W. Musser, Mitchell G. Reddish. *An Introduction to the Bible*. Nashville: Abingdon Press, 1991.

Bergant, Dianne and Robert J. Karris, gen. eds. *The Collegeville Bible Commentary*. Collegeville, MN: The Liturgical Press, 1989.

Boadt, Lawrence. *Reading the Old Testament*. New York: Paulist Press, 1984.

Broderick, Robert C., ed. *The Catholic Encyclopedia*. rev. ed. Nashville: Thomas Nelson Publishers, 1987.

Brown, Raymond, et al. *The New Jerome Biblical Commentary*. Englewood Cliffs: Prentice-Hall, Inc. 1990.

Coffey, Kathy. *Experiencing God with your Children*. New York: Crossroad, 1997.

_____. *Hidden Women of the Gospels*. New York: Crossroad, 1996.

The Community of Women and Men in the Church: A Study Program. The Advisory Committee, Study on the Community of Women and Men in the Church. World Council of Churches. New York: Friendship Press, 1978.

Craghan, John F. *The Psalms: Prayers for the Ups, Downs, and In-Betweens of Life*. Wilmington, DE: Michael Glazier Books, 1985.

Cross, F.L. and E.A. Livingstone, eds. *Oxford Dictionary of the Christian Church*. 2nd ed. New York: Oxford University Press, 1974.

Darcy-Berube, Francoise. *Religious Education at the Crossroads: Moving on in the Freedom of the Spirit*. New York: Paulist, 1996.

Dunning, James B. *Echoing God's Word*. Arlington, VA: The North American Forum on the Catechumenate, 1993.

_____. *New Wine, New Wineskins*. New York: Sadlier, 1981.

Ekstrom, Reynolds R. and Rosemary Ekstrom. *Concise Catholic Dictionary for Parents*. Mystic, CT: Twenty-Third Publications, 1982.

Finley, Mitch. *The Seeker's Guide to the Christian Story*. Chicago: Loyala, 1998.

Finley, Mitch and Kathy. *Building Christian Families*. Chicago: Thomas More Press, 1996.

Fuller, Reginald H. *Preaching the New Lectionary: the Word of God for the Church Today*. Collegeville, MN: The Liturgical Press, 1984.

Gentz, William H., gen. ed. *The Dictionary of Bible and Religion*. Nashville: Abingdon Press, 1986.

Good News Bible: The Bible in Today's English Version. Catholic Study Edition. Nashville: Thomas Nelson Publishers, 1979.

Halpin, Marlene. *Imagine That! Using Fantasy in Spiritual Direction*. Dubuque: Wm. C. Brown, Co., 1982.

Hamma, Robert M. *A Catecumen's Lectionary*. New York: Paulist Press, 1988.

Hiers, Richard H. *Reading the Bible Book by Book*. Philadelphia: Fortress Press, 1988.

Holmes, Urban T. *Ministry and Imagination*. New York: Seabury Press, 1976.

The Interpreter's Bible. George Arthur Buttrick, commentary ed. 12 vols. Nashville: Abingdon Press, 1955.

Irwin, Kevin. *Liturgy, Prayer and Spirituality*. New York: Paulist Press, 1984.

Kunkel, Fritz. *Creation Continues*. New York/Mahwah: Paulist Press, 1987.

Leech, Kenneth. *Soul Friends: The Practice of Christian Spirituality*. San Francisco: Harper & Row, 1977.

Lockyer, Herbert, Sr., gen. ed. *Nelson's Illustrated Bible Dictionary*. Nashville: Thomas Nelson Publishers, 1986.

McCauley, George. *The Unfinished Image. Reflections on the Sunday Readings*. New York: Sadlier, 1983.

McGinnis, Kathleen and James B. *Parenting for Peace and Justice: Ten Years Later*. New York: Orbis, 1990.

McKenna, Gail Thomas. *Through the Year with the DRE: A Seasonal Guide for Christian Educators*. New York: Paulist Press, 1987.

McKenzie, John L., S.J. *Dictionary of the Bible*. New York: Macmillan, 1965.

Merton, Thomas. *Bread in the Wilderness*. Collegeville, MN: The Liturgical Press, 1953.

Metzger, Bruce M. and Roland E. Murphy. *The New Oxford Annotated Bible with the Apocryphal/Deuterocanonical Books*. New Revised Standard Version. New York: Oxford University Press, 1991.

Murphy, Irene T. *Early Learning: A Guide to Develop Catholic Preschool Programs*. Washington, D.C.: National Catholic Education Association. 1990.

Myers, Allen C., ed. *The Eerdmans Bible Dictionary*. Grand Rapids, MI: Wm. B. Eerdmans Publishing Company, 1987.

The New American Bible. Nashville: Thomas Nelson Publishers, Catholic Bible Press, 1987.

Peck, M. Scott. *The Different Drum: Community Making and Peace*. New York: Simon and Schuster, 1987.

Perkins, Pheme. *Reading the New Testament*. 2nd ed. New York: Paulist Press, 1988.

Peterson, Eugene H. *Answering God: The Psalms as Tools for Prayer*. San Francisco: Harper and Row, 1989.

_____. *Earth and Altar: The Community of Prayer in a Self-Bound Society*. Downers Grove, IL: InterVarsity Press, 1985.

Pfeifer, Carl J. and Janaan Manternach. *How to Be a Better Catechist*. Kansas City, MO: Sheed and Ward, 1989.

Rahner, Karl, ed. *Encyclopedia of Theology: The Concise Sacramentum Mundi*. New York: Crossroad, 1982.

Schippe, Cullen. *Planting, Watering, Growing!* Granada Hill, CA: Sandalprints, 1990.

Senior, Donald, gen. ed. *The Catholic Study Bible*. New York: Oxford University Press, 1990.

Shea, John. *Stories of Faith*. Chicago: Thomas More Press, 1980.

Sloyan, Gerard. *Commentary on the New Lectionary*. New York: Paulist Press, 1975.

Spivey, Robert B. and D. Moody Smith. *Anatomy of the New Testament*. 4th ed. New York: Macmillan Publishing Company, 1989.

Stott, John. *Basic Introduction to the New Testament*. Grand Rapids, MI: Wm. B. Eerdmans Publishing Company, 1964.

Stuhlmueller, Carroll, C.P. *New Paths through the Old Testament*. New York: Paulist Press, 1989.

_____. *The Psalms*. 2 vols. Old Testament Message Series, nos. 21, 22. Wilmington, DE: Michael Glazier Books, 1983.

Vanier, Jean. *Community and Growth*. 2nd rev. ed. New York: Paulist Press, 1989.

Walters, Thomas P., project director. *Director of Religious Education: Yesterday, Today and Tomorrow*. National Catholic Education Association. Silver Burdett and Ginn.

Ward, Carol. *The Christian Sourcebook*. rev. ed. New York: Ballantine Books, 1989.

Westerhoff, John H., III. *Will Our Children Have Faith?* NY: Seabury Press, 1976.

Wigoder, Geoffrey, gen. ed. *Illustrated Dictionary and Concordance of the Bible*. New York: Macmillan Publishing Company, 1986.

Resources for the Seasons and Feasts

Carey, Diane and Large, Judy. *Festivals, Family and Food*. Gloucestershire, England: Hawthorne Press, 1982.

Dunning, James B. *Echoing God's Word*. Arlington, VA: The North American Forum on the Catechumenate, 1993.

Foley, Leonard, OFM, ed. *Saint of the Day: Lives and Lessons for Saints and Feasts of the New Missal*. Cinncinatti: St. Anthony Messenger Press, 1992

Halmo, Joan. *Celebrating the Church Year with Young Children*. Collegeville, MN: The Liturgical Press, 1988.

Luce, Clare Booth, ed. *Saints for Now*. Harrison, NY: Ignatius Press, 1993.

Mathson, Patricia. *Pray and Play*. Notre Dame, IN: Ave Maria Press, 1989.

Nelson, Gertrude Mueller. *To Dance with God*. New York: Paulist Press, 1986.

_____. *To Celebrate: Reshaping Holidays and Rites of Passage*. Ellenwood, GA: Alternatives, 1987.

The Oxford Dictionary of the Christian Church. ed. F. L. Cross. Oxford University Press, 1958.

Pennington, M. Basil, O.C.S.O. *Through the Year with the Saints*. New York: Doubleday Publishing, Image Books, 1988.

Pochocki, Ethel. *One-of-a-Kind Friends: Saints and Heroes for Kids*. Cinncinatti: St. Anthony Messenger Press, 1992.

Powers, Mala. *Follow the Year, A Family Celebration of Christian Holidays*. New York: Harper & Row Publishers, Inc., 1985.

Weiser, Francis X. *Handbook of Christian Feasts and Customs*. NY: Harcourt, Brace and World, 1958.

Resources for Prayer

deMello, Anthony. *Sadhana: A Way to God*. St. Louis: Institute of Jesuit Sources, 1978.

_____. *The Way to Love: The Last Meditations of Anthony deMello*. New York: Image Books, 1995.

Edwards, Tilden. *Living Simply Through the Day*. New York: Paulist Press, 1977.

Finley, Kathy. *Dear God: Prayers for Families with Children*. Mystic, CT: Twenty-Third Publications, 1996.

Glover, Mary and Rob. *Our Common Life: Reflections on Being a Spouse*. Chicago: ACTA Publications, 1998.

Kastigar, Carole. *For Our Children's Children: Reflections on Being a Grandparent*. Chicago: ACTA Publications, 1998.

Meninger, William. *The Temple of the Lord: and Other Stories*. New York: Continuum Publishing Group, 1997.

Owens III, Sherwood. *All Our Works Begun: Reflections on Being a Working Parent*. Chicago: ACTA Publications, 1998.

Pennington, M. Basil, O.C.S.O. *Awake in the Spirit*. New York: Crossroads, 1995.

_____. *Call to the Center: The Gospel's Invitation to Deeper Prayer*. New York: New City Press, 1995.

Strong, Dina. *Singular Ingenuity: Reflections on Being a Single Parent*. Chicago: ACTA Publications, 1998.

Taize Picture Bible. Philadelphia, Penn: Fortress, 1968

Learning Through Play

Fluegelman, Andrew, editor. *More New Games and Playful Ideas*. Garden City, NY: Doubleday, 1981.

_____. *The New Games Book*. New York: Pantheon, 1976.

Fry-Miller, Kathleen, Judith Myers-Walls, and Hanel Domer Shank. *Peace Works*. Elgin, IL: Brethren Press, 1989.

Gale, Elizabeth, editor. *Children Together*, Vol. 2. Valley Forge: Judson Press, 1982.

Glavich, Sr. Mary Kathleen, SND. *Leading Students into Scripture*. Mystic, CT: Twenty-Third Publications, 1987.

Griggs, Donald L. and Patricia Griggs. *Creative Activities in Church Education*. Nashville: Abingdon Press, 1984.

Griggs, Donald L. *20 New Ways of Teaching the Bible*. Nashville: Abingdon Press, 1977.

Halverson, Delia. *Teaching Prayer in the Classroom*. Nashville: Abingdon Press, 1989.

Hines, Rosemary Wesley. *The Idea Book*. Colorado Springs, CO: Meriwether Publishing, Ltd., 1981.

Orlick, Terry. *The Second Cooperative Sports and Games Book*. NY: Pantheon, 1982.

Peterson, Linda Woods. *The Electronic Lifeline: A Media Exploration for Youth*. Cincinnati: Friendship Press.

Priddy, Linda, Monte Corley, and Roy J. Nichols. *New Testament Bible Activities*. San Diego: Rainbow Publishers.

Rice, Wayne and Mike Yaconelli. *Play It!* Grand Rapids, Michigan: Zondervan Publishing House, 1986.

Schultz, Paul and Judith Wellington. *Caring for Creation*. Minneapolis: Augsburg Fortress, 1989.

Smith, Judy Gattis. *26 Ways to Use Drama in Teaching the Bible*. Nashville: Abingdon Press, 1988.

Vos Wezeman. *Peacemaking Creatively through the Arts*. Brea, CA: Educational Ministries, Inc., 1990.

Ward, Elaine M. *All About Teaching Peace*. Brea, CA: Educational Ministries, 1989.

_____. *Be and Say a Fingerplay*. Brea, CA: Educational Ministries, 1982.